SIMPLE
TIBETAN BUDDHISM

A Guide to Tantric Living

WITHDRAWN

SIMPLE
TIBETAN BUDDHISM

A Guide to Tantric Living

C. Alexander Simpkins Ph.D. • Annellen Simpkins Ph.D.

Tuttle Publishing
Boston • Rutland, Vermont • Tokyo

First published in 2001 by Tuttle Publishing, an imprint of Periplus Editions (HK) Ltd, with editorial offices at 153 Milk Street, Boston, Massachusetts 02109.

LIBRARY OF CONGRESS CATALOGING-IN-PUBLICATION DATA WILL BE FOUND
AT THE END OF THIS BOOK.

Distributed by

<table>
<tr><td>USA</td><td>JAPAN</td></tr>
<tr><td>Tuttle Publishing</td><td>Tuttle Publishing</td></tr>
<tr><td>Distribution Center</td><td>RK Building, 2nd Floor</td></tr>
<tr><td>Airport Industrial Park</td><td>2-13-10 Shimo-Meguro, Meguro-Ku</td></tr>
<tr><td>364 Innovation Drive</td><td>Tokyo 153 0064</td></tr>
<tr><td>North Clarendon, VT 05759-9436</td><td>Tel: (03) 5437-0171</td></tr>
<tr><td>Tel: (802) 773-8930</td><td>Fax: (03) 5437-0755</td></tr>
<tr><td>Tel: (800) 526-2778</td><td></td></tr>
</table>

SOUTHEAST ASIA
Berkeley Books Pte Ltd
130 Joo Seng Road
#06-01/03
Olivine Building
Singapore 368357
Tel: (65) 280-1330
Fax: (65) 280-6290

First edition
06 05 04 03 02 01   10 9 8 7 6 5 4 3 2 1
Printed in the United States of America

We dedicate this book to our parents, Carmen and Nathaniel Simpkins and Naomi and Herbert Minkin, and to our children, Alura L. Simpkins Aguilera and C. Alexander Simpkins Jr., and to all the true bodhisattvas whose compassionate actions have helped improve our world.

Carmen Z. Simpkins's abstract expressionist paintings suggest mood, movement, and mysticism. Simpkins has been painting for seventy-five years. Her first solo show took place in Camden, Maine, in 1962 at the Broadlawn Gallery. She has exhibited throughout the world, and her works are in private collections in Europe and America. She continues to display her work at her galleries in Sebastian, Florida, and Clinton, South Carolina.

CONTENTS

INTRODUCTION

The Dalai Lama has been very much in the public eye in recent years, both as the winner of a Nobel Peace Prize and as a spokesman for freedom and compassion. Still, many people do not know about the long and colorful tradition he leads, Tibetan Buddhism.

Tibetan Buddhism is a form of Buddhism that, through a method of inner transformation, offers an active way of enhancing life. It is transformation that is accomplished through various methods and techniques that engage the mind, the senses, and one's behavior. With these practices, a person learns to experience a vibrant life filled with color and beauty.

Modern culture has pushed to secularize life, to separate the spiritual from the material. But Tibetan Buddhism believes there is nothing that can't be sanctified, nothing that can't be a symbol of the spiritual,—that can't awaken in us our deeper, spiritual natures. Everything we do, even the simplest daily routines, can be meaningful. And then, when life is over, we can learn how to face death with a clear, calm mind, even look upon death as an opportunity to transform consciousness.

Virtue, Tibetans believe, can be taught, and they have devised a carefully worked out system that trains the mind to become enlightened. It takes time and effort, but it can be done. And anyone can do it. Virtue is altruism: love, kindness, compassion, and tolerance. Tibetan Buddhism teaches people how to free themselves from those things that interfere with expressing their own best qualities. The ultimate goal in Tibetan Buddhism is to become a compassionate, caring human being who can live fully and happily, whatever the circumstance, enriched by everyday life as an expression of nirvana—enlightenment.

ABOUT THIS BOOK

Simple Tibetan Buddhism is written to introduce you to this form of Buddhism and to show you how you can adapt it to enhance your life. Part I traces the background and development of Tibetan Buddhism to the present day, highlighting pivotal people who helped to make it what it is. Part II explains important themes and methods. Tibetan Buddhists are very pragmatic in that the techniques they have developed are intended to help people travel to enlightenment more quickly and fully. Part III introduces practical exercises so you can try aspects of Tibetan Buddhism for yourself. You can experiment with meditations and learn how to apply them in your own life. Ultimately, you can discover your deeper self and live in accord with it.

HOW TO USE THIS BOOK

Meditate! The meditations in this book can be learned by anyone, but they do take practice. Do not be discouraged if some exercises are difficult. If you have trouble with one method, try another. The book offers a variety of techniques to speak to all sorts of people.

Be honest with yourself! If you sincerely and patiently try to correct yourself as you go along, you will progress. For those who would like to pursue this path more comprehensively, there are numerous Tibetan Buddhist organizations that will welcome and teach you further.

Even though enlightenment is the goal, keep in mind that it is not something beyond you or outside of what and who you are. The Path is one of self-discovery, of bringing out the innate potential that is already present. May you enjoy the journey.

PART I

Tibetan Buddhism in Time

We can reach beyond our lives
Into times we do not know
To the center of the mandala
Our spirit will inevitably go
—C. Alexander Simpkins

With three ways to approach its teachings, Tibetan Buddhism encompasses the entire evolution of Buddhism. The first Way, Hinayana, began with Buddha's method of finding personal liberation. Mahayana, the second Way, developed Buddhist liberation to include other people and universal compassion. The third Way, Vajrayana, offered new methods to reach enlightenment. Though Vajrayana's roots are in India, it was most fully developed by the Tibetans. Vajrayana shares with Mahayana the goal of universal compassion but believes that by following the tantric path, people can accelerate the journey to enlightenment. As you read Part I, may the vision of Tibetan Buddhism appear for you, beckoning you to embark on your own journey of inner transformation.

Buddha-to-be-Sakyamuni. Late 10th century, Pala period,
India, Granite. Gift of the Asian Arts Committee, San Diego
Museum of Art

CHAPTER 1

The Three Wheels of Buddhism: Hinayana, Mahayana, and Vajrayana

One thing is made up of many parts and in itself does not exist. There is nothing that is not made up of many parts. Without the idea of "one thing" the many does not exist and without the idea of existence there is no non-existence.

—Nagarjuna in T. Freke, *The Wisdom of the Tibetan Lamas*

HINAYANA: THE FIRST WAY

According to the Hinayana tradition, Buddhism began with the profound awakening of one man, Gautama Siddhartha (563–483 B.C.). The son of a king, Siddhartha grew up sheltered from any worldly problems yet with a sensitive and caring nature. He lived lavishly and married one of the most beautiful girls in the kingdom. But Siddhartha felt a restlessness he could not explain. When he saw his subjects suffering from illness, old age, and death, he felt compelled to seek solutions to the despair and hopelessness shared by all humanity. He left his comfortable life behind to search for answers. He spent six years living in the woods with a group of ascetics who practiced a form of austere yoga. Siddhartha fasted for long periods, engrossed in meditation in order to free himself from the suffering of embodied existence. But even as he came close to death from starvation and exposure, he was no nearer to a cure for suffering. After taking some food and feeling renewed, he sat under a bodhi tree and meditated through the night. As the sun rose over the horizon he had a full awakening. He now understood how to solve the problem of suffering and resolved to help others.

Buddha's story can be an inspiration to all, for he showed tremendous perseverance and sincerity in his search for a spiritual path.

BUDDHA'S MESSAGE

Buddha found his enlightenment not from complete abstinence nor from uncontrolled gratification. The true light came between the two extremes. His solution was a path he called the Middle Way. He encouraged people to use their common sense, claiming that by staying fit in mind and body, you have the best chance of finding enlightenment.

Buddha taught his solution as the Four Noble Truths. This, according to the Tibetans, constitutes the first vehicle of dharma. The First Truth is to realize and accept the fact that living is suffering. We may have happy and fulfilling experiences, but they are impermanent. Once this is realized, we can recognize the origin of suffering that comes from our cravings and desires—the

Second Truth. The Third Truth is that we can overcome suffering by giving up our cravings and desires. Buddha agreed that this may be difficult to do, so he set down a demanding but clear-cut path for us to follow. The Fourth Truth is the Eightfold Path: right views, right aspiration, right speech, right behavior, right livelihood, right effort, right thought, and right contemplation. (For an in-depth description of the truths and path, see *Simple Buddhism*.)

Buddha spent the remaining forty-five years of his life traveling and teaching this method. He drew many followers during his lifetime. Following his death, his talks and ideas were written down and were eventually gathered together in the *Tripitaka*. Composed in Pali, an early Indian language, these works included the sutras, sermons taught by Buddha and his teachers; the Vinaya or rules of the order; and the Abhidharma, commentaries on the sutras.

MAHAYANA: THE SECOND WAY

The Second Way came after Buddha's death. Some followers felt that Buddha's path was too limiting. It offered enlightenment only to those individuals willing to give up their personal lives to become monks, *arhats*. The goal to become completely free from desires was a solitary one. A new ideal emerged: the bodhisattva, or enlightened being. Instead of staying isolated in nirvana, bodhisattvas turn away from enlightenment, and return to the world to help others until every person is enlightened.

The Mahayana expanded the meaning of the Four Noble Truths. The goal was not simply to overcome suffering but to wake up from illusion. We live our daily lives in a dreamlike state. When we overcome ignorance by correcting our thinking, we come to a new understanding about the nature of reality: emptiness.

This doctrine of emptiness was a new idea of the Mahayana. Real wisdom is the recognition that everything in our world is ultimately without individual essence, and enlightenment is the intuitive realization of this. Our everyday life (*samsara*) and enlightenment (*nirvana*) are One. And we find enlightenment in and through daily life. This is the true essence of Buddhism, and it is found in all activities.

Buddha was also changed. No longer thought of as an individual person, Siddhartha, Buddha was now a cosmic being, a symbol of enlightenment. He became eternal and omniscient, representing the absolute wisdom of enlightenment.

Two Sects of Mahayana Buddhism: Madhyamika and Yogacara

Mahayana Buddhism is divided into two major schools: Madhyamika, the Middle Way, and Yogacara, Mind Only.

Nagarjuna, the founder of Madhyamika, was considered one of the greatest Mahayana thinkers. He reinterpreted the Middle Path by stating that it is not simply a choice between luxury and austerity, but rather something that should be viewed more philosophically. The Middle Way is a path between, on the one hand, the belief in the existence of things, and on the other hand, the belief that nothing exists. The first is based on superstition and faith, the second is founded on nihilism.

Nagarjuna pointed out that no position is certain. What we are left with is a path that takes us between existence and nonexistence, reality and illusion: neither and yet both. In this way, we escape from the delusion of dualistic, either/or thinking. Unlike Aristotelian logic, which says that either a thing is (it exists) or is not (it does not exist), Buddhist logic says things are *and* they are not. From the perspective of enlightenment, this paradox disappears. On the relative, everyday level of reality, things do indeed exist. But from the enlightened perspective of the absolute, everything is empty of any real, lasting existence. Both and neither are true at the same time.

The other major Mahayana sect in India, the Yogacara school, was founded by two brothers, Vasubandu and Asanga, in A.D. 400 and had a profound influence on Mahayana, and later, Tibetan Buddhism. The word *cara* means practice. Thus, the Yogacara school used yoga in its attempts to reach enlightenment.

The Yogacarins believed that everything we know and experience is a manifestation of the mind—their famous formula was Mind Only. There is no objective world outside of the mind that perceives it. The very intelligence that we use to perceive our world is our own little drop of universal mind. The world is entirely illusory. All the methods we use to measure it and conceptualize it are like trying to grip air in your hand. The real nature of the world is empty, nothingness. This can be very liberating, because if the world is illusion, then the enlightened mind has no boundaries. It can deconstruct what seems to be indestructible. Nothing is there to obstruct us; nothing stands in our way.

Consciousness is like the ocean, vast and deep. Waves are like thoughts. They are not different from the ocean, yet they are not the entire nature of the ocean either. They are simply one part of it. Similarly, our thoughts are never all of consciousness, of Mind, yet they are always part of it. Thus we cannot hope to understand the ocean if we only know waves.

Enlightened wisdom is described in positive terms as pure thought. This differed from the earlier Hinayana idea of nirvana as extinguishing desires. If reality is nonreality, then it is an ultimate state of nonstate. This is a positive conception. There is an Absolute Mind, even if it is empty of substance.

THE VAJRAYANA: A NEW WAY

The Vajrayana, or Diamond Vehicle, was absorbed by the Tibetans into their form of Buddhism, and incorporates both Hinayana and Mahayana. It uses rational thinking and one-pointed concentration to open the mind to new abilities and to the fuller development of potential. According to the Dalai Lama,

> *What is unique about the third turning is its presentation of particular medita-*
> *tive techniques aimed at enhancing the wisdom realizing emptiness and its dis-*
> *cussion, from a subjective perspective, of various subtle factors involved in a per-*
> *son's experience of that wisdom. (Tenzin Gyatso 1995, 27)*

In Tibetan Buddhism, enlightenment is the goal, but an enlightenment that is based in this life, now, as symbolic. We can partake of the Universal Mind through the mind and body that we are. Tibetan Buddhism guides people toward this positive conception of nirvana by using special meditations. Ritual and visualizations give the practitioner an experience of the enlightened state of mind.

Tibetan Buddhist doctrines unite a seemingly diverse group of practices so as to offer a variety of ways to truth and enlightenment. These practices involve the use of tantras and yoga. The word *tantra* refers to a varied set of practices that foster the realization of enlightenment, but it is also used to describe the sutras on tantric practices. Yoga, on the other hand, is a way to focus concentration while performing tantras to enhance Buddhist practice even more. These methods employ all the senses, training and developing them into tuning forks for enlightenment. Sounds (*mantras*), visual symbols (*mandalas*), and gestures (*mudras*) help direct and intensify the Way.

Tibetan Buddhists do not avoid words or concepts. Thoughts and ideas, for them, are linked to a higher reality. In Zen Buddhism, enlightenment is wordless, beyond knowledge and thought. By contrast, Tibetan Buddhists utilize thought and ideas to lead to the experience of a higher reality.

The individual mind, seen as an individual symbolic essence, is a function of the Universal Mind. All practices are intended to lead to this transformation, the gemstone, or jewel, of higher consciousness.

Avalokitesvara, the patron Buddha of Tibet, Four-armer
Avalokitesvara, Buddha of Mercy, Applied Thangka, 18th century,
Tibet, Silk and glass beads, The Newark Museum/Art Resource, N.Y.

CHAPTER 2

Buddhism Turns Toward Tibet

One mind pervading all life. It is the primal state, that goes unnoticed. It is brilliant, boundless intelligence that is ignored. It appears everywhere and always, but is not seen.
—Padmasambhava in T. Freke, *The Wisdom of the Tibetan Lamas*

The tapestry of Tibetan history interweaves myth with fact, religion with politics. Primary in this tapestry is Buddhism. Tibetans mark their important events around the time of the introduction and development of Buddhism in their country. Religion is so closely woven into everyday life that Tibetans consider spiritual realms just as real as material ones. They think symbolically and metaphorically, readily moving between relative and absolute levels of reality, often without making any distinctions. Such interlacing may be unfamiliar to Westerners, but it presents new possibilities for interpreting this interesting and colorful people.

MYTHIC BEGINNINGS

The true origin of the Tibetan people is uncertain, but the myth is clear. Originally, Avalokitesvara (Kannon to the Japanese and Kuan Yin in Chinese), a bodhisattva of compassion, lived alone in Tibet, incarnated as a monkey. Far away, in another part of Tibet, lived a wildly emotional and lustful ogress. When the ogress discovered she was alone, she cried loudly. The monkey heard her pitiful cries and felt compassion for her suffering. He found her, and they had six human children. These offspring were the first Tibetans. In mythical terms, Tibetans are the missing link in evolution, from ape to human.

Tibetans believe that much of their early cultural and political evolution came from India. According to legend, the first king of Tibet grew up in India. He was slightly deformed at birth and felt rejected by his family. So he left home as a young man and journeyed all the way to the Yarlung valley in Tibet, located southeast of Lhasa. The Tibetans noticed his gentle spirit, not his deformed body, and asked where he came from. Not speaking their language, he tried to communicate with gestures and pointed up to the sky. They interpreted this to mean he was sent from heaven to rule them. They made him their chief and gave him the name Nyatri Tsenpo, heavenly born lord. Nyatri Tsenpo introduced many advances from Indian civilization, including building the first house. He is known as the first ruler of the first dynasty, the Yarlung dynasty.

BUDDHISM TAKES HOLD

The early people of Tibet were warring tribes who personified nature and the forces of life in spirits and deities, both friendly and threatening. Their Bon religion gave these spirits form in roles and rituals. By the seventh century, the Yarlung king Songsten Gampo (A.D. 618–650) united the tribes into an empire. The Tibetan army ventured outside its borders to conquer parts of China, India, and Burma (in A.D. 635). In all the countries they attacked and conquered, the troops noticed two things: the countries were more advanced than Tibet and Buddhism flourished. The king decided that Buddhism was the key.

To remedy this, the king imported two wives for himself, one from China and the other from Nepal. Both were devout Buddhists. Through these marriages, he brought Buddhism to Tibet and a spiritual conversion for himself. He built the Jokhang Temple for his Nepalese wife and the Rampoche Temple for his Chinese wife. Both became centers for Buddhism in Tibet.

The king also recognized that his country lacked a universal written language. He had a language brought back from India, establishing the standards for Tibet's native tongue.

The Bon religion's many deities maintained their strong hold on the daily life of Tibetans, with the people trying to please the good deities and appease the evil ones. Buddhism, lacking gods, seemed weak in comparison.

King Trisong Detsen (790–798) decided to change this apparent imbalance by bringing the wise Indian Buddhist scholar Santaraksita to teach in Tibet. The king's ministers, firm believers in Bon, opposed the visit. When Santaraksita's journey was impeded by several natural disasters, the Tibetans saw it as a sign that the visit angered their gods.

Not to be stopped, the king sought out the Indian Buddhist Padmasambhava, who had a reputation as a great and powerful sorcerer. Padmasambhava practiced a form of Buddhism that incorporated tantra, a mental and ritual practice that enhanced personal powers. When combined with Buddhism, it was believed to speed practitioners on the Buddhist path. Padmasambhava accepted the challenge to overcome the angry Bon gods. On the way to Tibet, he encountered a ferocious snowstorm. He took shelter in a cave and meditated deeply. The snowstorm subsided and he arrived safely, easily defeating the demons. The people of Tibet were so impressed that they accepted his presence and welcomed Santaraksita's return. Padmasambhava's teachings developed into the first Tibetan Buddhist sect, known as Nyingma, or Old School.

In 775, Padmasambhava and Santaraksita established the first Buddhist monastery in Tibet, Samye. The buildings were arranged in a mandala pattern, symbolizing one of the tantric practices that uses mandalas to deepen Buddhist insight (see Chapter 7).

Buddhism continued to grow and develop from the influence of the Indian, Nepalese, and Chinese scholars who came to Tibet. Many Buddhist texts were translated during this time, helping to spread the understanding of Buddhism.

Two forms of Buddhism evolved: one from India and the other from China. The Indian method believed in slowly accumulating wisdom and skills in meditation, a practice called gradual cultivation. This method combined Buddhist principles with tantric practices. The approach from China believed that understanding comes in a flash of insight, sudden enlightenment. This form, influenced by Buddhism combined with Chinese Taoism, is best known as Zen (Japan) or Ch'an (China).

The Lhasa intellectuals felt that the two approaches were incompatible. But they were not sure which one was best for Tibet. The king decided to hold a public debate between a prominent representative from each method. The winning approach would be taught in Tibet. Everyone gathered to watch the duel of wits. After a heated discussion back and forth, the King chose the master from India. A gradual cultivation incorporating both Mahayana and tantra became the nationally accepted form of Buddhism in Tibet.

The third religious king, Rebachen (reigned 815–836) gave Buddhism lavish support but neglected his political duties. As a result, his ministers became angry with him, feeling Buddhism was distracting him from his duties. They had him assassinated and placed Lang-Dharma (reigned 838–842) in power. This king was devoted to the older Tibetan religion, Bon. He attacked Buddhism, sending Buddhist monks into hiding. Outwardly, Buddhism seemed to be destroyed, but the seeds remained. Intrigue and power struggles continued, leading to the assassination of Lang-Dharma. His death marked the end of the long-standing Yarlung dynasty and sent Tibet into chaos. Tibet remained isolated, never again to stretch an imperialist hand outside its borders.

RETURN OF BUDDHISM

The second dissemination of Buddhism came from the Indian monk Atisa (982–1054), one of the greatest teacher-reformers of Tibet. He was from a dying breed in India, where Buddhism was waning, yet he had a great influence on Tibetan Buddhism. He was able to influence the king and bring new life to Buddhism. His writings are filled with good advice to common people and kings alike:

> *Behave like one with eyes with regard to your own faults but as the blind with regard to the faults of others. Avoid arrogance and egoism and always meditate on the void. . . . Purify all actions, physical, oral, and mental, and never indulge in any sinful act. (Chattopadhyaya 1967, 19–20)*

Atisa encouraged people to live morally and to selflessly sacrifice for others. His teachings started the Kadampa sect that eventually became the Gelukpa sect. As Buddhism became firmly rooted in Tibet, new branches began to grow.

MONGOL INFLUENCE

During the thirteenth century, the Mongols were conquering the known world. In 1240, under the leadership of Godan Khan, the grandson of Genghis Khan, the Mongols attacked Tibet. Godan became acquainted with the Tibetan Buddhist leader from the Sakya tradition, Gurga Gyeltsen Bel Sangpo (1182–1251). He liked Buddhism and decided to convert. The two men set up a joint government arrangement they called priest-patron between the Sakya priests, known as lamas, and the Mongol khans. Thus Buddhism continued to develop in conjunction with Mongol rule.

Mongol influence lessened in the early 1300s and Tibetans took back the full leadership of their country. They returned to the older Tibetan rites and customs that integrated with Buddhism, which had been forbidden during Mongol rule.

ORIGINS OF THE DALAI LAMA

The Sakya sect became less central as a newer, reform school grew, the Gelukpa, System of Virtue. This was the first eclectic school to draw its roots from Tibet, not India. One of the Gelukpa leaders, Sonam Gyatso (1543–1588) visited the Mongol chief Altan Khan. Although all priests in Tibet were called lamas, Altan conferred on Sonam Gyatso the title Dalai Lama, which meant "Ocean of Wisdom." Altan Khan decided to retroactively make Sonam Gyatso's two predecessors the first and second Dalai Lamas, and Sonam Gyatso was to be the third. The authority for this title was conferred by the Mongols, but eventually the Dalai Lama would become the sole leader of the country without any outside authority to authenticate the title.

The fifth Dalai Lama, Ngawang Losang Gyatso (1617–1682), was a talented, dynamic individual who had a profound influence on Tibet and Tibetan Buddhism. He had the rare ability of being competent as both statesman and religious teacher. He united Tibet politically into one country and spiritually under the Gelukpa sect. Although he maintained the priest-patron relationship with the Mongols, he gradually shifted the source of the Dalai Lama's power from the Mongols to the Tibetan patron-saint Avalokitesvara. In this way, the Dalai Lamas came to be seen as incarnations of Avalokitesvara. He built a palace, the Potala, in Lhasa, where the Dalai Lamas of the future would live and rule, making Lhasa the spiritual and political capital of Tibet.

THE MANCHU INFLUENCE

In 1664, the Manchus conquered China and established the Ch'ing dynasty, which maintained control of China until 1911. Although the

Manchus continued to be linked with Tibet, like the Mongols before them, the interactions were often vague and irregular. Tibet became more isolated from its neighbors. Although the Dalai Lama tradition continued, a truly strong leader did not come along until the thirteenth Dalai Lama.

The thirteenth Dalai Lama, Tupden Gyatso (1876–1933), was a competent, somewhat controversial leader who had a lasting influence on Tibet's course as he carried it into the twentieth century. During the early years of Tupden Gyatso's reign, the Manchu general Chao Erh-feng tried to take control of Tibet. Though he met with resistance from the people as he marched to Lhasa, the unarmed farmers could do little to stop him. The Dalai Lama, warned of the invasion, fled to India. When Chao finally arrived at the Tibetan capital to negotiate surrender, he found no Tibetan government to negotiate with! Chao's quest for control was finally put to an end when the Manchu government fell to the Chinese Nationalists in 1911. Chao was executed by China's new government, and the Dalai Lama returned to rule his country.

The thirteenth Dalai Lama's experiences showed him that Tibet had become too isolated from the international community, militarily weak, and socially underdeveloped. He decided to alter Tibet's direction. He created an army and encouraged young Tibetans to study in England as a way to introduce them to Western-style thinking. Both plans met with some opposition from the monastic establishment, but the wheel of modernization had begun to turn.

CONCLUSION

Tibet's history shows how, despite great adversity through the ages, Tibetan Buddhism's ancient wisdom has been a great source of strength. Carefully passed along from guru to student, these timeless insights inspire us today as they have inspired people in the past, proving that there is hope for the inner development of all humanity.

Padmasambhava in the form of Guru Drakpoche, Pictured
embracing his female consort, Thangka, late 17th century, Tibet,
The Newark Museum/Art Resource, N.Y.

CHAPTER 3

The Spokes of the Wheel: The Four Tibetan Sects

The notion that the whole universe with the totality of its phenomena forms one single whole in which even the smallest element has an effect upon the largest, because secret threads connect the smallest item with the eternal ground of the world, this is the proper foundation of all tantric philosophy.
—Walt Anderson

Indian Buddhism was eclectic when it was brought to Tibet. Students learned traditions from both Hinayana and Mahayana. They used all resources available, including sutras and tantras drawn from many different Indian Buddhist sects. As Tibetans integrated these learnings into their culture, they formed their own schools with a uniquely Tibetan flavor. Four major traditions arose in Tibet to guide people in Tibetan Buddhist practice: Nyingma, Kagyu, Sakya, and Gelukpa.

NYINGMA SCHOOL

Nyingma was the first school and is often referred to as the Old School to set it apart from the other three, which are considered New Schools, based in newer Tibetan translations and interpretations. The founder of Nyingma was Padmasambhava, the first Buddhist to influence Tibet. He not only showed Tibetans how to practice Buddhism, but he also introduced tantric practices, which were his specialty.

Nyingma has nine sets of teachings, organized and guided by the practice of certain tantras: three common, three outer, and three inner. These teachings guide and help transform the conduct, beliefs, thoughts, and feelings of practitioners into higher consciousness. The first six tantras are similar to the other sects. The first three are Hearer Vehicle, Solitary Realizer Vehicle, and Bodhisattva Vehicle. The three associated with outer tantras are action tantra, performance tantra, and yoga tantra. The three inner tantras are called Mahayoga, Anuyoga, and Atiyoga and help people realize the true nature of mind, cutting through appearances to reality. Sudden insight leads to enlightenment. The goal becomes the path, and the path is not reliant on images or visualizations.

Nyingmas clear their minds and focus attention on the present moment of experience without conceptualizing what the object of experiencing is. Distorted, inaccurate perceptions of phenomena transform to accurate perceptions of reality's true nature, a union of luminosity and emptiness free from opposition and polarities without distinctions that could confuse or deceive.

Nyingma teaching is designed to lead to the actualization of this awareness in everyday life.

Deity Yoga is an important part of the Nyingma school. Through Deity Yoga, practitioners can identify with and incorporate the best qualities of their guru and the many great Buddhas throughout time. The deities of this school are Samantabhadra, the primordial Buddha, and Vajradhara, the emanation of Samantabhadra.

SECRET DOCTRINES: TERMA

Nyingma utilizes *terma*, documents, artifacts, and images that had been hidden by their original teacher, Padmasambhava. The terma fill out and develop further the concepts and practices of Nyingma.

The terma were supposed to be found and revealed at appropriate times by disciples called *tertons*, gifted bodhisattvas who are believed to be emanations of Padmasambhava himself. *Dakinis*, female wisdom beings, help guide the tertons in finding these important writings and objects. Once the terma is discovered, the tertons transmit the teachings. According to tradition, terma were hidden throughout Tibet, with spells on them to prevent their being uncovered prematurely. Terma are continually being found and released by tertons, who, using secret keys to uncover and decode them, rediscover and reinterpret the doctrine in ways appropriate to the time and place. In this way, the Nyingma teachings continue to evolve and adapt so they can guide humanity regardless of present or future conditions and circumstances. Terma will be discovered and disseminated when they are needed.

SAKYA SCHOOL

Sakya descended from the Khon lineage, a people who claimed to be derived from celestial beings. The Khon were followers of the Indian yogin

Virupa, who taught Drogmi Shakya Yeshe (992–1074). Drogmi Shakya Yeshe journeyed from Tibet to India to study and brought back to Tibet teachings from Virupa on the Kalachakra, the Path and Fruit, as well as the doctrines of other Indian masters. There is only one authoritative text for this sect, Virupa's *Vajra Verses*. Most of the teachings were passed along orally, as secret traditions transmitted directly from teacher to student.

Khon Koncheck Gyelpo, one of Virupa's disciples, built a monastery and called it Sakya, which translates as the Gray Earth, the color of the ground in Tsang Province of Central Tibet on which this monastery was built. Gyelpo took this as an auspicious sign, based on a well-known vision of Atisa, who envisioned gray earth with two black wild yaks grazing near it. The Sakya sect took its name from this monastery, and the Sakya family continued this lineage.

The Sakya sect had a tradition of rule in Tibet before the Dalai Lamas. The Sakya leader Gurga Gyeltsen Bel Sangpo (1182–1251) had a great reputation for wisdom and was invited by Goden Khan, grandson of Genghis Khan, to Mongolia to give lectures on Buddhist teachings. In 1253, after Sangpo died, Kublai Khan invited Sangpo's nephew, Drogen Chogyal Phagpa, to his court. Phagpa developed a script to write Mongolian, which led Kublai Khan to honor him. Kublai Khan declared Buddhism the state religion of Mongolia, and gave Phagpa the spiritual and secular rule of Tibet's three provinces. The Sakya clan retained this position for the next one hundred years.

The Sakya's central teaching is called Lamdrey (pronounced Lam - bras), which translates to mean "The Path and Its Fruit." This doctrine is a synthesis of the paths and fruits of both the inner and outer teachings. Path and Fruit teachings direct the student to embrace existence in everyday reality, samsara, as inseparable from nirvana. Path and Fruit doctrine teaches that when Mind is obscured, it forms samsara; when clear, it shows nirvana.

Mind is a union of luminosity and emptiness. Since Mind is not located in any place, when looked for it cannot be found—not in your body, nor outside it, and not in the brain. Yet when you seek it, there is no place the Mind is not found. Thus Mind is not anywhere in particular. This is known as non-abiding, one of the characteristics of Mind. The Mind cannot be known by what it is, but it can be known by what it is not. The essence transcends any attempt to categorize it and allows you to see through it. Thus the characteristic of luminosity can be applied to the Mind. This unity of luminosity and emptiness is a fundamental construct in Sakya doctrine.

Sakya training leads to three levels of degree, similar to graduate school in theology. First comes scholarly study for the first degree, followed by tantric work for advanced degrees.

KAGYU SCHOOL

The Kagyu sect of Tibetan Buddhism includes both meditation and philosophical training. Kagyu practitioners extend and develop the mind and visionary capacities.

This sect emphasizes the passing along of insight, from teacher to student, called Guru Yoga. The guru is the source of guidance, values, and instruction, giving very deep wisdom to the student. Guru Yoga requires a strong identification with the teacher as spiritual master. This permits the teacher to transmit teachings directly from his mind to the student's mind. Thus, there is exacting concern by Kagyu practitioners for the direct line of transmission of teachings.

The name Kagyu means "teaching lineage." Marpa Choyi Lodae (1012–1099) and Khyungpo Nyaljor (978–1079) were the founders. Marpa was a translator who traveled three times to India and four times to Nepal for teachings. He studied with 108 spiritual masters and adepts, most notably Naropa.

The lineage began in India with Tilopa (988–1069), who received his teachings from the Indian master Vajradhara. Tilopa passed his teachings to Naropa, who underwent trials and tribulations for twelve years under Tilopa's guidance. Naropa's enlightenment taught him to develop clear, open self-awareness, like the clear skies. Naropa taught Marpa the six doctrines of tantric yoga that he had learned from Tilopa. These doctrines were yogas of the transference of consciousness, illusory body, dream state, clear light, inner heat, and bardo. Naropa also taught Marpa the Kalachakra tantra, which involves the construction of an elaborate mandala, symbolizing the world of phenomena and enlightenment. The mandala is a diagram that encodes most of the fundamental insights of Tibetan Buddhism.

Milarepa (1040–1123), Marpa's student, became one of the greatest Tibetan Buddhists teachers. As a young man, Milarepa was disinherited from his family fortune and studied black magic to get revenge. After following this course for a time, he realized he had done great wrong and sought Tantric Buddhism to help him escape the negative consequences of his bad karma. Milarepa learned the six yogas from a female partner of Marpa. He combined the teachings he learned from Marpa with Mahamudra Yoga, the yoga of the Great Symbol. Milarepa became famous throughout Tibet as a culture hero, reputedly possessing great yogic powers. He wrote poetic songs about his insights.

The mountains are a joyous place full of flowers.
Monkeys play in the forest trees.
Songbirds sing and insects swarm.
A rainbow shines both day and night.

Summer and winter bring soothing rain.
Spring and autumn bring shifting fog.
Solitary in simple clothes, I am happy here
because I see the Clear Light
and contemplate the emptiness.
I am delighted by appearances
because my body is free from bad actions.
A strong mind wanders contentedly
and is naturally cheerful.
(Milarepa in Freke 1998, 74)

Milarepa's student Gampopa (1079–1153) had disciples who evolved new lines of their own, but all are quite similar in basic doctrines. Gampopa synthesized Mahamudra, Naropa's six yogas, and the stages of the path from the Kadampa order. Many subsects formed from his disciples and their disciples, resulting in many subtle variations in Kagyu, but all remained based on Mahamudra teaching applied to the practice of the six yogas of Naropa.

The core of Kagyu is Mahamudra Yoga, a meditative discipline that puts into practice Yogacara and Madhyamika philosophies. Since all is Mind and Mind is empty, all possible content is empty of absolute meaning and reality. Many varieties of practice can lead to enlightenment, and so the experience of dreaming, of body warmth, even of death itself are all opportunities to actualize enlightenment as a lived and experienced awareness. This is how tantric yoga can lead to enlightenment here and now, in this body and life. The Kagyu use their carefully trained awareness to transform this body into Buddha. Buddhahood then becomes a means of helping others.

GELUKPA SCHOOL

The Gelukpa tradition, founded by Tsong Kha Pa (1357–1419), is an eclectic school based on the Kadampa tradition of Atisa. All the earlier traditions were integrated together to utilize the best from each. Modern Kagyu doctrine is an important part of the Gelukpa eclecticism, which has included the Mahamudra and the six yogas of Naropa as systems of training, along with the Kalachakra. Gelukpas integrate the use of the intellect along with meditation and philosophy.

Tsong Kha Pa received lay ordination at the age of three and got novice vows at seven! He studied many traditions, including medicine, from more than a hundred teachers all over Tibet and India. Eventually, he taught thousands of pupils. He also wrote widely and collected eighteen volumes of writings on all aspects of Buddhist teaching. His successors headed monasteries that subsequently became teaching institutions, combining scholarship with spiritual training.

The Dalai Lama tradition arose within the Gelukpa sect when the third in the lineage, Sonam Gyatso was given the name by the Mongol Khan (see Chapter 2). Each Dalai Lama is considered an incarnation of the patron saint of Tibetan Buddhism, Avalokitesvara. They are found as a young child, based on signs and intuitions. Over time, the Dalai Lamas became the political head of state as well as religious ruler.

The student goes through fifteen to twenty years of study to achieve three possible levels of accomplishment. Debate on sutra and tantra are part of the curriculum. A graduate has the equivalent of a Ph.D. in Buddhist philosophy and is called a Geshey. The geshey may graduate and continue to study, teach, or retire into meditative seclusion. India's branch of Tibet's government in exile has four Gelukpa monasteries and a tantric college to maintain their scholarly, honorable tradition.

Gelukpas believe that everyone is born with a little enlightenment, possessing intuitive wisdom from childhood. From this small beginning people can develop and learn, and become fully enlightened. The First Dalai Lama advised: "Practice without bias toward the objects; Embrace everything and cherish all from the heart." (Druppa 1993, 158)

Walter Evans-Wentz gazes out from the vista of his Sacred
Mountain Cuchama in San Diego County, California. Courtesy of
D. G. Wills Books, La Jolla, California.

CHAPTER 4

Modern Voices

My religion is kindness.
—His Holiness the Dalai Lama

WESTERNERS WHO INTRODUCED TIBETAN BUDDHISM

One of the first Westerners to visit Tibet and give first-hand accounts of what he experienced was Englishman L. Austine Waddell. He became interested in studying Buddhism, which he considered one of the great living religions of the world in 1879. During his work for the Indian Medical Service, he was stationed in India, where he was able to delve deeper into his studies. He was involved in some excavations that revealed actual relics of the Buddha himself, convincing Waddell that Buddha was a real historical person. By chance he was sent to Tibet, to Dorjeling, and seized this opportunity to delve into the little known Buddhism of Tibet, then known as Lamaism. He learned the language and conversed directly with lamas and natives.

His book, *The Buddhism of Tibet or Lamaism*, was the product of these years of study. Published in 1894, this book portrayed Tibetan Buddhism as a mysterious and magical religion that he found to be strange and often bizarre. The book is filled with detailed descriptions of what he saw and experienced, but because he had no precedence to follow, his understandings were often limited and tinged with prejudice. However, he did do a great service in bringing this tradition to the attention of the West.

Walter Y. Evans-Wentz, (1878-1965) was the American who first popularized Tibetan Buddhism in the West by his translations with extensive commentaries on four major Tibetan texts. His most well known is the *Tibetan Book of the Dead*.

Evans-Wentz had a spiritual nature from childhood. He attended Stanford University and then Jesus College in Oxford, England. Continually in search of deeper insights, he traveled extensively in Europe and India. He eventually found his way to Tibet where he was attracted to the deeply spiritual atmosphere. He studied with the Tibetan lama Kazi Dawa-Samdup who was headmaster of a school and an official interpreter for India. Evans-Wentz learned some of the Tibetan language as well as Sanskrit. He collaborated with Lama Samdup and continued the work after the lama died, to become one of the first English-language translators (*lotsavas,* as translators of sacred texts are called in Tibet). He returned to the United States to live at the Keystone Hotel in San Diego, California, so he could be close to the main branch of the San Diego public library. He spent many years there working on his research and translations.

Evans-Wentz had always wanted to open a spiritual center. He almost purchased property to do so in India, but was prevented by the outbreak of World War II. Piece by piece, he purchased Mount Tecate, known to the Native Americans as Sacred Mountain Cuchama located on the Mexican border in San Diego County. He believed that mountains symbolized the quest for enlightenment. He said, "There is more to climbing a 'celestial' mountain than conquering perpendicular footage. Upon returning, men report having found a true peace of mind on Sacred High Places, sometimes akin to that of a spiritual initiation (Evans-Wentz 1981, xi)."

Unlike his Western predecessors, Evans-Wentz developed a deep sympathy for Tibetan Buddhist mysticism, allowing him to render the texts and his explanations in an objective and inviting style. According to Govinda, a leading Tibetan scholar and friend, Evans-Wentz approached his work "in the spirit of true devotion and humility, as a sacred trust that had come into his hands through generations of initiates, a trust which had to be handled with the utmost respect for even the smallest detail" (Govinda in Evans-Wentz 1960 lxiii).

Today there are many great scholars and translators who are bringing the wisdom of Tibet to the West. A great deal of Tibetan art has also been brought to the west to be preserved. We are fortunate to have so many sources to draw from as this profound and colorful tradition opens new ways of experiencing to us today.

THE CURRENT DALAI LAMA, TENZIN GYATSO

The fourteenth and current Dalai Lama, Tenzin Gyatso (1935-) is a very human and likable person with a broad vision for his country, Tibetan Buddhism, and the world.

The Dalai Lama has opened himself and Buddhism to all who would open themselves to receiving its fruits. Many actors and actresses have become attracted to Tibetan Buddhism. They find in Tibetan Buddhism a method that they can relate to. Tantric practices allow people to integrate this philosophy into their lifestyle. Deity yoga, which encourages people to identify with and become the best qualities imaginable is a natural development for the actors and actresses who are accustomed to taking on roles, even becoming them for a moment in time.

People who meet the Dalai Lama often are surprised by his sense of humor and humility. Part of the Dalai Lama's charm lies in his disarming lack of egotism. He says of himself, "I am just a simple monk with no exceptional wisdom to impart." Yet he is a person of matchless conviction and genuine compassion. Thomas Merton, the famous Catholic theologian said after talking with the Dalai Lama, "The Dalai Lama is a most impressive person. He is strong and alert, bigger than I had expected... a very solid, generous, and warm person, very capably trying to handle enormous problems" (Merton, 1968).

Early Years

Tenzin Gyatso was discovered as a young child to become the fourteenth Dalai Lama. His training began at the age of six. For eighteen years he was carefully taught and groomed for his position. He delved into every aspect of Buddhist studies. Throughout his schooling, he approached his learning with a curiosity and openness that he retains to this day.

The young king's schedule was demanding, and he was expected to be serious and disciplined. But as a normal youth, he had interest and curiosity about everything and everyone around him. He spent many hours talking to people, from the lowest servants to high-ranking teachers. Another interest he had was tinkering with mechanical devices. He repaired anything he could find on the palace grounds. The only three automobiles in all of Tibet were garaged there, and the young Dalai Lama worked long hours on their repair. Much to the dismay of his elders, the boy took one of the cars out for a drive. At that time, there were no paved roads in all of Tibet. The drive on the bumpy terrain was less than successful when the brakes failed! The Dalai Lama continues to enjoy fixing things. His brother Tendzin Choegyal said, "One of the Dalai Lama's greatest finds in recent years was super glue—second, in fact only to the more recent discovery of super-glue remover" (Gluckman, 1996).

The Dalai Lama was very curious about Western culture. His sheltered life offered few glimpses into Western ways. Heinrich Harrar had escaped a World War II prison camp by climbing the Himalayas to Tibet. The Dalai

Lama welcomed him as a friend and a teacher about the ways of the outside world. Harrar built a movie theatre where the Dalai Lama watched many American films. He especially enjoyed the adventures of his favorite movie hero, John Wayne. Today he has little time for television or movies, except for a brief daily update from BBC World News, but he values the time he spent exploring Western culture with his friend Harrar.

At the end of his formal education the Dalai Lama was given a rigorous three-month oral examination in front of thousands of monks and scholars. He took preliminary examinations at three Tibetan monastic universities in 1958. The final exam was given in 1959 at Jokhang Temple in Lhasa. Questioned from morning till night on logic, philosophy, and Buddhist principles, the Dalai Lama's years of study were thoroughly tested. He passed with the highest academic honors, attaining a degree equivalent to a Ph.D. in Buddhist metaphysics.

Political Leader

While the Dalai Lama was growing up, a regent had been appointed to run the Tibetan government. But a political crisis brought on by a Chinese invasion of Tibet forced the fifteen-year-old Dalai Lama to take on the full power of his position, three years short of the traditional age to do so. He accepted the political power of his position and all the weighty decisions that it entailed.

The Dalai Lama chose to negotiate with the Chinese and spent nine years trying to bring about a peaceful co-existence. He visited China in 1954 and returned hopeful after the long voyage to Beijing. But over time the situation deteriorated as negotiations broke down. He fled Tibet in the middle of the night on March 31, 1959, to carry on his efforts from the safety of India.

The Dalai Lama set up a government in exile in Dharamsala, India, where he resides today. The Indian government helped him set up schools, handicraft factories, hospitals, orphanages, monasteries, and cultural institutions. Today there are fifty-three Tibetan settlements in India. The Dalai Lama's government has been involved in numerous publications as well as charitable organizations to help foster Tibetan culture along with Tibetan Buddhism.

Spiritual Leader

The Dalai Lama's great inner strength, drawn from Buddhism, allows him to love his enemies as much as his friends. He feels his calling to help not just his own country, but to guide all humanity toward more spiritual living.

> *My message is the practice of compassion, love, and kindness. These things are very useful in our daily life, and also for the whole of human society these practices can be very important. (Dalai Lama, 1988)*

The Dalai Lama has engaged in many open dialogues with people from all around the world. He expresses great respect for Western perspectives and has shared Tibetan Buddhist ideas with many Westerners. He said in his autobiography:

> *With the ever-growing impact of science on our lives, religion and spirituality have a greater role to play in reminding us of our humanity. There is no contradiction between the two. Each gives us valuable insights into the other. Both science and the teachings of the Buddha tell us of the fundamental unity of all things. (Tenzin Gyatso 1990, 270)*

Through his deep commitment to his spiritual values, he carries on an ancient tradition, first preserved within his isolated mountain country and now being shared with the world. He believes that the qualities of love and compassion can be developed by anyone. The international community has recognized his efforts by awarding him the Nobel Peace Prize in 1989.

The Dalai Lama is open to all belief systems and encourages people to stay with their own religion. He believes that Tibetan Buddhism can help people to enhance and intensify their personal spirituality, whatever that may be. He said, "I further believe that all religions pursue the same goals: those of cultivating goodness and bringing happiness to all human beings. Though the means might appear different, the ends are the same" (Tenzin Gyatso 1990, 270). He hopes to enlighten all with loving kindness and compassion.

PART II

Tibetan Buddhist Themes

We live in a world of symbols
From our birth past when we die
The circle of life continues
Linking earth with the inner sky
—C. Alexander Simpkins

Although Tibetan Buddhism shares many of the themes of other forms of Buddhism, it draws upon different methods. When you follow the tantric way, mandalas are more than mere pictures, and mantras reach beyond simple sounds. You learn to engage all your senses and mental faculties throughout every facet of life. Open your mind to new possibilities, and you can expand your understanding of yourself.

CHAPTER 5

Using Yoga and Tantra to Attain Enlightenment

*Regardless of whether your practice is elaborate or short, above all,
it should be effective in bringing about some kind of transformation,
a change for the better, within you.*
—His Holiness the Dalai Lama

Tibetan Buddhism integrates Mahayana Buddhism with two ancient methods: yoga and tantra. Yoga and tantra are usually done separately but are synthesized together in Tibetan Buddhism as complimentary practices.

YOGA

Yoga is typically thought of as an Indian practice, but there are variations in China, Tibet, and other cultures. Traditionally, yoga is a tool to unite mind and body with focused attention. Purposeful and goal-oriented, yoga was one of the first applications of meditation, and all subsequent systems of meditation share in one or more methods of practice.

Yoga was described in the epic *Bhagavada Gita, Blessed Lord's Song*. In this famous dialogue between Krishna and Prince Arjuna, Krishna outlines a series of methods for disciplining the mind, body, and emotions to a task. Arjuna faced a war where he must take sides in a battle even though he had family members on both sides, an uncomfortable situation. Through his dialogue with Krishna, Arjuna's military situation is reinterpreted into a committed, disciplined, ethical act. The epic explains how to apply focused concentration in order to successfully deal with life at its most difficult moments.

Later, the *Yoga Sutras* of Patanjali (150 B.C.) systematized yoga in a series of statements. Patanjali claimed he was gathering ancient practices that predated written records. These brief aphorisms describe the main yoga practices of concentration and meditation and how to practice them. Patanjali also points out that great mental powers can be gained by doing yoga.

MEANING OF YOGA

According to *Webster's Dictionary*, yoga is the "method by which to harness the body to the soul, and the soul to the universal Soul." Yoga emphasizes concentration of attention, leading to immersion and subsequent loss of personal limitations in order to transcend the individual self, to find the greater true self. A second, less-known definition of yoga is simply meditation (Evans-Wentz, 1958). Viewing the two definitions together fills out the true meaning and usage of yoga.

This use of focused thought joins consciousness with whatever it is focused on. The disciplined concentration of mind leads to yoking or uniting the individual consciousness to the universal collective unconscious or Mind. Specific practices are believed to lead to specific results, but nonspecific changes in consciousness take place, too. By training the mind in meditation, yoga leads to mental control. Tibetan Buddhism adapted yoga as a way to train awareness for Buddhist enlightenment.

YOGA IN TIBETAN BUDDHISM

Tibetan Buddhism uses consciousness and reason to deliberately focus thought and attention. According to Tibetan Buddhism, *maya*, ignorance, is due to misconceptions. To help bring about enlightened perception, Tibetans use focused awareness, and yoga is the discipline that is applied to control and direct the mind—that is, to focus awareness. This method of meditation allows the practitioner to attain union with the One Mind (Evans-Wentz, 1958).

Buddhist yoga differs from Hindu yoga in terms and techniques but not in the essentials. The aim of Hindu yoga is to join part consciousness to whole consciousness, individual with universal. In Buddhism, to merge an individual consciousness with the ocean of Buddhism is to relate to nirvana, to find and follow the light.

Nagarjuna's Madhyamika philosophical assumptions and Yogacara's Mind-Only philosophy are used in Tibetan Buddhism as bases for yoga practices. Focused meditation clears the mind of unenlightened concepts. The true essence is like a clear mirror behind all phenomena; all things exist by it and in it, part of the true, perfect body of Buddha. Through yoga meditation, the Tibetan Buddhist can experience this essence, thereby becoming One with nirvana.

TANTRA

No one knows the exact origin of tantra. Tantra techniques are very ancient and some form is found in many ancient cultures. The Sanskrit word *tantra* implies continuation, weaving together, but there is no real single definition. Tantra includes many sets of techniques, usually action-oriented, to weave together mind and body.

Techniques that developed in India were also used as part of Hinduism. Around the seventh century, tantric techniques were combined with Buddhism. Buddhism had been developing in India for more than a thousand years, with large complex monasteries and impressive statues. But Buddhists felt that some practitioners were losing sight of the original spiritual simplicity that Buddha had intended.

Tantric practices were introduced as a reform movement to help bring Buddhism back to its roots. Ordinary people could perform tantric rituals as part of their daily lives, as these practices would point them directly to the deeper spiritual qualities within. All anyone needed was sincere commitment, not wealth, education, or position. In this way, tantra helped to revitalize Buddhism and return it to the everyday person.

Tantric practices also offered a way to achieve Buddhist enlightenment in one lifetime. Some of the older Indian forms of Buddhism believed that it took many eons of time and infinite rebirths before a person could be enlightened. But according to Mahayana, enlightenment is possible in this life, in this body. Tantra gives a deliberate method to focus action directly toward enlightenment. Practitioners could empty themselves of ego and open their hearts to true reality. In tantric practice, a guru was often sought to point out the path, to help practitioners avoid obstructions and to guide them toward enlightenment.

Left-Handed Tantra and Right-Handed Tantra

There are two types of tantras, the left and the right. Left-handed tantras in Tibetan Buddhism are known by several other names: Diamond, Adamantine, or Thunderbolt Vehicles. But all tantric vehicles collectively are known as Vajrayana. This method is called a vehicle because, like an automobile or train that takes us to our destination, following it carries the practitioner on a speedy path to enlightenment.

The diamond is the hardest substance known. It is pure, clear, powerful, and unbreakable. The Vajrayana vehicle incorporates the qualities of the diamond, integrating the method with insight in an indestructible and perfect union. The body and mind of those skilled in these practices are transformed. The successful practitioner becomes a diamond being.

Right-handed tantra, The Mi-Tsung, School of Mystery, was systematized by Amoghavana (705–774), preserved in China, and eventually introduced to Japan as Shingon Buddhism where it merged complex symbolic tantric practices with Japanese Buddhism. The right-handed tantra form used mandalas and circle diagrams as symbols. Tibetan Buddhism incorporated them as well.

The word *tantra* is also used for writings that describe tantric practices. The *Guhyasamaja Tantra* is one of the first writings of the Vajrayana, originating in approximately A.D. 300 but not developed into a system until A.D. 600. A second Nagarjuna (A.D. 600–650), known as Guru Nagarjuna, was the founder of the left-handed school. Living in northern India, he taught tantric practices. Royal patronage helped Tantric Buddhism to develop. During the Pala dynasty (A.D. 750–1150), tantric methods became incorporated with the Mahayana sutra, the *Prajnaparamita, Wisdom Sutra*.

Tibetan Buddhists use the dramatic symbolism of the diamond and thunderbolt not as something to be taken literally but to inspire practitioners through stories and descriptions of methods. Everything becomes an opportunity, a symbol of transformation.

Vajrayana is for strong-willed, compassionate people who want to help others and are determined to achieve enlightenment as quickly as possible. It takes determined effort to develop the spiritual capacity to pursue the difficult path of tantra.

Integration of Yoga with Tantra in Tibetan Buddhism

Yoga has been combined with tantra to actualize the potential for enlightenment. Tantric systems of visualization are like maps that orient the mind and body toward nirvana. Yoga concentration is the focused beam that illuminates the map. Once well trained in yogic concentration, practitioners perform tantric practices that transform the physical experience of their bodies into the body of enlightenment. In using the power of will and concentrated attention in combination with these secret techniques, skilled practitioners are said to gain mastery over life and death.

Tibetan Buddhism also incorporates Karma Yoga, the yoga of work. Tibetan Buddhism encourages the use of all experiences to evoke enlightened states of mind. Practitioners learn to use their senses and emotions as windows to higher consciousness. Symbols open the doors of perception so that nirvana can be experienced.

This mind, this body, this world is the way to nirvana. There is no other. The higher synthesis is to live and work while continuing on the quest for enlightenment. Honest work need not interfere with spirituality if the correct attitudes are maintained. Contradictions dissolve into a synthesis that is both individual and universal. Our daily struggles—is our work meaningful or just a means for paying the bills, are the overall efforts of life and work as we evolve in our careers spiritual—are all grist for the mill. We can use our lives to heighten awareness. Our goal-oriented actions are threads that weave the cloth of our spiritual evolution. Our intention and commitment to enlightenment transforms the ordinary into the extraordinary. Life becomes magnificently colorful and multi-textured, as the drama of nirvana unfolds.

Tantric practices do not exclude using analytic forms of reasoning as a way to learn and experience. There is no limit or boundary to restrict thought. Through highly developed concentration that follows the tantric journey, practitioners deconstruct their world. They see the world as a function of the concepts of mind. Therefore, the mind can free itself from concepts. This becomes possible for the fully disciplined and advanced practitioner, conferring great benefits.

Tantra's ultimate intention is to experience enlightenment by living fully within our given mental, emotional, and physical capacities. What begins with deliberate focus of conscious attention, the gross levels of mind, becomes natural undistracted attention of the unconscious, subtle levels of mind. Abilities develop step by step as mental skills improve. Eventually, practitioners are said to perform miraculous feats, transcending the limitations of space and time and overcoming the physical laws of gravity—even overcoming death itself.

Use of Language in Tantras

Tibetan Buddhism uses language symbolically to point to higher truths. Called intentional language, exact meanings, the literal or objective meanings, are not the point; the aim of the language is to imply or suggest higher truths. Gurus hide the meaning of terms behind obscure words to protect their students, to keep them from being misled. The guru also uses language to hide the secrets of the sect from non-initiates.

Since the logic of Mahayana is non-Aristotelian, a thing is not defined by its being or nonbeing. Language used to describe things will not delineate boundaries and perimeters; instead, a word points toward the unknown through symbols, a word means what it means to mean—all meaning is empty of constant content. Hiding the exact meaning reveals the deeper truth. Sexual symbols, peaceful and wrathful deities, and other powerful symbols are used to speak to the subtle unconscious mind that can respond sensitively, discovering greater attunement.

Tantric Practices

Tantric practitioners are initiated into the secrets of the sect with a series of rituals and ceremonies. First, practitioners take vows to sincerely commit themselves to a moral, compassionate life. They recite mantras (sounds) and visualize mandalas (images) to activate and focus consciousness. An example of a sound is the phrase "Form is emptiness, emptiness is form," a core statement from the *Heart Sutra*. Used as a focus for meditation, the words are chanted regularly to clear the mind and set consciousness on the path to enlightenment. The practitioner's mind can then be guided by focused attention toward realizing higher truth. Since the word and its sound are One with what they signify, their use in mantric yoga is a natural extension of Buddhist concepts. Even simple syllables may be concentrated on as mantras for meditation. For example, "Om Mani Padme Hum" is chanted for many purposes (see the mantra and mandala chapters for details).

Deities are used to focus consciousness and activate associated meanings and symbolic attributes within the practitioner. Tantric rituals and yoga offer an opportunity to enlarge the range of consciousness when practitioners first visualize a guru sitting before them communicating great wisdom and then imagine that they become the guru.

Tantrism permits the use of many symbolic things as skillful means, help for the path. Tantric Buddhism aims to transform the basic experiences of life using words, thoughts, feelings, and actions as symbols, to lead the student to the Clear Light of the Great Symbol (Mahamudra) where all these things are no longer needed.

OM MANI PADME HUM, Traditional script for this important mantra.

CHAPTER 6

Mantra: The Sound of Enlightenment

Om is the symbolic word for the infinite, the perfect, the eternal.
—Lama Anagarika Govinda

Tibetan Buddhists believe that the nature of the universe is expressed in sound, in mantra. The mantra is a powerful way to focus and attune consciousness.

The word *mantra* comes from the Sanskrit roots *manas,* mind, and *tra,* tool. Latin has a similar root word, *mens,* which means mind. Mantras are tools of the mind. The essential core, the unifying sound of enlightenment, of samsara with nirvana is mantra. Om is the original mantra; brought over from Hinduism, it was expanded and now stands at the beginning of every mantra in Buddhism. Om symbolizes the wholeness of things, the infinite and perfect. Chanting a mantra is a way to focus attention and direct oneself into union with enlightened consciousness.

When people unused to Tibetan Buddhism listen to the monks chanting their mantras, they think the sounds are strange. But if a Tibetan monk listens to common American sounds, a football team in training, for example, the player's grunts and yells would sound strange to the monk! The players and coach use these sounds to evoke feelings of strength and focus on the field. These sounds do not seem strange to them. We all become accustomed to our own sounds, and use them to evoke experiences and meaning. A girls' hockey match may have many characteristic sounds that the girls use to focus their efforts. A high school dance has ritualized movements and sounds, meaningful to the participants, that evoke and channel feelings and actions. Such "cultural mantras" put us in touch with the spirit and feelings central to our culture and society. The mantras of Tibetan Buddhism stimulate spiritual experiences that are pointed toward inner transformation.

Mantras utilize dynamics that are natural. We may spontaneously yell with happiness or anger, shout to release emotion or stress, or sing when happy. We hear our names and respond. Some people hum instinctively while going about their work. But mantras use this natural capacity deliberately, to focus attention and consciousness at will.

Certain sounds are fundamental to the human condition. Sounds tell us about what is happening. According to linguists, some sounds are universal to all children, worldwide. These sounds, uttered soon after birth, are the basis for language and communication. Sounds direct us toward reality; they get our attention and resonate with the frequencies of the universe.

In mantric theory, the universe is a function of Buddha, codifying his words that express the fundamental essence. Words and sounds are not separate from the essence of reality; they are at One with reality. By chanting the appropriate sounds and combinations of sounds, the corresponding meaning or experience is evoked.

Hindu theory has long held that the universe is in harmony. Modern physics does not disagree. Each particle, each molecule, and so each object has its own vibration, its own frequency as a unity. A great singer can shatter a glass by singing a single note in harmony with the frequency of the glass. A platoon of soldiers who march over a bridge always assign one soldier to be out of step so that the vibration they generate will not shake the bridge apart. A great martial arts master can stop his opponent with only a shout. Properly used, mantras have great potential.

> *Mantras do not act on account of their own "magic" nature, but only through the mind that experiences them. They do not possess any power of their own; they are only the means for concentrating already existing forces—just as a magnifying glass, though it does not contain any heat of its own, is able to concentrate the rays of the sun and to transform their mild warmth into incandescent heat. (Govinda 1970, 28)*

Mantras have been used since the beginning of religion in one form or another. The mantric form of Buddhism in China was known as Chen-yen, which translates as True Word School. Even the first line in the book of Genesis evokes a mantra: "In the beginning was the word and the word was God." We are forever linked to mantras, in one form or another. So we might as well use them.

OM MANI PADME HUM

Om Mani Padme Hum, which translates as "Hail to the Jewel of the Lotus," is the root mantra of Avalokitesvara, Tibetan Buddhism's patron bodhisattva. The universe begins with Om and ends with Hum. The world's vibrations are epitomized in this mantra, especially Avalokitesvara's mantra, which evokes the unified essence of the buddhas.

Chanting this mantra is not based on reasoning, since rational concepts and ideas lead away from direct perception. Mantras develop inner vision. This mantra does not point consciousness to any object or referent. This mantra opens a window, shows an image, like a reflection in a mirror, of the essential of the universe. Mantras provide an experience to listen to, so the practitioner can hear the universe itself with direct awareness.

Om Mani Padme Hum is chanted regularly by practitioners to clear the mind and set consciousness on the path to enlightenment. Practitioners chant to fill the mind and thereby shut out distractions. Focus of attention is used to direct the practitioner's mind toward higher truth, in accord with Tibetan Buddhist principles.

Each syllable has meaning, both literal and symbolic. Symbols may be used to evoke an experience. In the six yogas of the Kagyu sect, mantric syllables are pictured within the complex visualization of chakras (centers of spiritual energy in the body) in order to direct consciousness to experience the circulation of heat and to achieve the altered states the practitioner aims to bring to awareness. These practices are used to promote healing.

Each syllable of the mantra is also a seed syllable of one of the buddhas of the directions of the universe. The sound of reality is expressed as HUM. The consonant H—hhhhhhhhhh—in HUM is like breathing out. UM—ummmmmmmmmmmm—at the end signifies the unity, the vibration of the universe.

The mantra's sound, its image, and the meaning-essence is identical with the sound and essence of Mind, which is reality itself. Therefore, visualizing mantras is important, part of saying them, because the power of the mantra is in its use as a sign and not just as a mechanism of concentration or something you just listen to. The sound and its image are not two separate things. The mantric vision is a unity. Thus, each mantra syllable invokes a corresponding bodhisattva while it activates a related chakra or spiritual center of consciousness, and focuses awareness, all together.

Each syllable may be concentrated on as symbols for meditation. For example, Om Mani Padme Hum is chanted for many reasons. The word and sound are one with what they signify, so their use in mantric yoga is a natural extension of Buddhist concepts. As Buddha approached death, he was asked what sutras were to be authoritative, and he replied, "Whatever is well-spoken is the word of the Buddha." Mantric practitioners take this literally.

Wheel of Existence, Thangka, 18th or early 19th century,
Eastern Tibet, Colors on cotton cloth, The Newark Museum/Art
Resource, N.Y.

CHAPTER 7

Mandala:
Higher Consciousness
by Visualization

*The choice of the circular shape for a pattern intended to depict the
universe is not accidental. The circle, the only figure that does not
single out any particular direction, is used spontaneously everywhere to depict objects whose shape is uncertain or irrelevant,
or to depict something that either has no shape at all, any shape, or
all shapes.*
—Rudolf Arnheim, *Toward a Psychology of Art*

Mandalas are ancient, beginning long before Tibetan Buddhism used them,
dating back to prehistory. Every culture has some form of mandala that has

been adapted to a variety of philosophies. The psychoanalyst Carl Jung used mandalas extensively in his work. He encouraged his patients in deep analysis to express themselves and their transformation in the pictorial imagery of mandalas, and his patients often created their own personal mandala to do just that. He found that the practice facilitated analysis and higher synthesis of the personality. Each patient's mandala was unique and showed the individualizing of this phase. He believed that the pattern is archetypal, fundamental to our inherited collective unconscious, and symbolic of the central pole of the Self, the axis of the inner universe.

MANDALA AS CIRCLE

The word *mandala* in Sanskrit means circle, and mandalas are circles. In early Buddhism, they were simple circles. Later, the circles became more complex, with geometric patterns of squares and triangles within the circle.

The mandala, as a circle, is found extensively in our everyday lives. We do not realize its all-pervasiveness, but the circle, square, and triangle that make up the patterns of our world are basic to Tibetan Buddhism. We take a circle's meaning for granted, but we never notice the form which evokes that meaning. The form is itself real.

It is remarkable how many of the basic, essential, core activities and meanings of our lives take place in the shape of the mandala—the circle. The plates off which we eat our food—basic to life—are circular. The pots and pans we cook in are circular. The spoon, the first eating instrument used to feed a child, is a circle. The hats that cover our heads start with a circle. We speak of the cycles of our lives, of the seasons—the earth itself is circular. When circles and lines are combined, all the letters of the alphabet become possible.

The circle is often used in religious symbols. A circle within a square is a symbol of God in Christianity. The wheel of Buddhist dharma is a circle, with the eight spokes of the Eightfold Path radiating from its central hub, empty space. The yin-yang of Taoism is a circle. Zen's symbol for enlightenment is the empty circle.

Science reveals that the dynamics of physical properties incorporate aspects of mandala structure. One of the most startling examples is the benzene ring, a circular link of carbon atoms, fundamental to all life. We take this for granted, as part of the design of our world. But mandala symbols offered timeless truths before scientists had made their discoveries.

THE CIRCLE CONTINUUM

Western concepts of mathematics use linear equations. Lines are central; they have a beginning and an end. Geometric diagrams use lines combined in different ways to make many different shapes. A mandala is simply a line with no beginning and no end, a mysterious quality. The concepts of Tibetan Buddhism are organized around this central view of the circle continuum. All of life is a continuum, from birth, to death, to rebirth. The continuum evolves from a center, yet it is a center without substance, and this is how these concepts refer to each other continuously.

TYPES OF MANDALAS

In Tibetan Buddhism, two types of mandalas evolved. One depicts the Buddha in the center, usually meditating, representing emptiness, the core of Buddhism. We think of the center as profound—our math begins with simple arithmetic and its number line, based in zero, and proceeds outward to advanced math concepts. Zero makes higher mathematics possible: Similarly, from the center the mandala takes form.

Surrounding the meditator are an array of buddhas, bodhisattvas, gods, and goddesses. Sometimes mandalas represent architectural designs of monasteries, with the four directions represented by squares within the circle, doorways that are guarded by watchful deities. Symmetry is found in the outer patterns of symbolic meaning and the boundary around it. The two-dimensional representations are multicolored, giving a three-dimensional effect.

The second type of mandala depicts a model of the universe. Known as the wheel of existence or wheel of life, these mandalas show the entire continuum of life, death, and the period between. A personified image of death often sits above the circle, watching over. The designs are complex, filled with the many facets of both conscious and unconscious life.

In all mandalas, the shapes and symbols visually communicate a code of meaning that allows a special relationship between the concepts and the viewer.

ENTERING THE MANDALA FOR TRANSFORMATION

Mandalas are incorporated into practice as part of the meditative process. In a very real sense, transformation may be conceived through the mandala.

The mandala expresses a certain tension and movement, as a form. We tend to orient to the center, the source of the circle. The well-constructed mandala induces the observer to imagine motion to the center, to enter and be channeled.

A mandala's circle has an inside and an outside boundary. Tibetan Buddhists speak of entering the mandala, which implies that the mandala is not just a map: The mandala is the opening to another dimension of being. The mandala shows the Way and is the Way. Entering the circle, entering the mandala, involves initiation into a process of transformation. A guru leads the practitioner in the experience.

Entering the mandala gives an experience to transform within, to let go of limitations and expand potential. We play many roles in life. Some can transform us, especially when the role transcends the person who plays it. The stories we tell and act out in life become sources of insight. By playing roles, we learn about ourselves and our world. We discover what fits and what does not, what we can do and what feels uncomfortable and inhibiting.

Entrance into the mandala begins from the peripheries of the Buddhist doctrine and gradually penetrates to one's own center. What begins as a role becomes part of who you are, to be one with the core of your being. The mandala is the self in transformation, in the process of change.

The root word of mandala, *manas*, means mind. Since the mind is central to Tibetan Buddhism, the mandala helps to crystallize and diagram the unconscious, giving a clear depiction of the inner mind.

IMPORTANCE OF SYMBOLS

It is only possible to live the fullest life when we are in harmony with the symbols; wisdom is a return to them. It is a question neither of belief nor of knowledge, but of the agreement of our thinking with the primordial images of the unconscious. (Jung, 1981, 402–403)

The mandala serves as an important system of symbols, carefully pointing to the dynamics of reality. Tibetan Buddhists use the mandala as a central, organizing principle for a practice that represents the main concepts of Tibetan Buddhism. Thus, mandalas are more than mere drawings, though a drawing or painting may represent it. They are symbols of the Great Symbol: our world and all existence.

Mandalas show a perspective of reality that helps the practitioner perceive reality more deeply. The exact symbols help guide the practitioner toward the correct experience. The mandala is an archetypal experience.

We of the West also use symbols to point to reality. We use geometric diagrams to describe and predict reality. We call it mathematics, vectors, quantum numbers. We are making sense of the world just as the Tibetans use symbols to understand theirs. The content of our symbols is different, but the truth is in the symbolism itself, in the process of symbolizing, not in the form and content of the symbol. A great forest is more than just the type of trees that make it up. Similarly, the ocean is more than merely salty water and the movement of waves. At the same time, the forest *is* also the individual trees in it. The ocean *is* salty water with waves. But it is also so much more. We can calculate the forces, measure the wave height, and the tides. Using our instruments, we can measure the height of the trees, categorize the types of trees, count them, and so on. All these calculations are symbolic operations that tell us more about the world.

Tibetan Buddhists measure with the instrument of their consciousness; their minds intuitively grasp reality and its parameters. They use the mystical diagrams of mandalas and the visual concepts of consciousness contained within to apprehend the events likely to occur.

Mathematicians can also predict likely events, only they use the diagrams of their models. We can calculate the unseen forces that will shake apart a bridge unless steps are taken to carefully balance these forces. Similarly, the adept trained in Buddhist yogas and tantras *senses* the hidden forces within reality and can *sense* how to balance them.

Symbols are used to point out and describe how to act, how to accomplish things. Tibetan Buddhism uses symbols to point out how to act and what to do, to function and accomplish the wisdom of enlightened higher consciousness. Mandalas permit the use of symbols, as skillful means, to help on the path.

Vajravarahi (Vajrayogini), 16th century, Tibet, Central region, Silver with gold, turquoise inserts and pigments, The Newark Museum/Art Resource, N.Y.

CHAPTER 8

Dakini: Wisdom From Our Feminine Side

I must practice devotion to women
Until I realize the essence of enlightenment.
—*Candamaharosana Tantra*

Women have always had a prominent role in Tibetan Buddhism. Even though Tibet was male-oriented, Tibetan Buddhism considered the female perspective an essential component for reaching enlightenment. Women were given both a real, worldly role as partners in practice as well as a symbolic role as keepers of enlightened wisdom. Both men and women were seen as equally capable of enlightenment, and they could discover it together.

DAKINIS AS ENLIGHTENED FEMALE BEINGS

Women were given a symbolic role in the pantheon of Tibetan Buddhist deities and were called dakinis. The word *dakini* translates as "sky walker," a woman who flies. Because sky symbolizes the void, a dakini can be understood as one who travels in the void. The void is the enlightened realm, and she who travels in the void is enlightened. Through much of traditional Tibetan Buddhist literature, dakinis are viewed as women of great wisdom who are often sought for their insight and understanding.

Dakinis have been given important and varied roles in Tibetan Buddhism. People often say that behind every great man is a great woman. Many Tibetan Buddhist stories show how men were guided on their path by an enlightened woman. In one famous story, a devoted practitioner named Saraha tried very hard to understand enlightenment. He thought that the best way to meditate would be to seek absolute silence, far away from anyone or anything. An outspoken dakini criticized him harshly for trying to discover enlightenment away from the world. "Don't sit at home and don't go out into the forest," she told him. "Just recognize mind wherever you are!" On hearing these words, Saraha realized that the dakini was right and altered his practice accordingly. This advice is very similar to the doctrine of Zen Buddhism, which teaches that everything we do—walking, sleeping, eating—is an opportunity for meditation and correct understanding.

Another dakini advised a poor practitioner named Kantali, who barely made a living by scavenging rags and piecing them together to sell. The dakini advised him:

> *Envision the rags you pick and stitch as empty space. See your needle as mindfulness and knowledge. Thread the needle of compassion and stitch new clothing for all the sentient beings of the three realms. (Shaw 1994, 57)*

Vajrayogini: The Divine Dakini

Tibetan Buddhism removes the boundaries from between the divine and the mundane. Dakinis are no exception. Vajrayogini is a primary deity dakini included with the many symbolic figures of Tibetan Buddhism. She is usually pictured as a beautiful woman, red in color, with long, flowing black hair. She dances in the sky, holds a skullcup filled with ambrosia, and expresses an uninhibited and passionate personality.

Vajrayogini is a symbol for the best qualities of womanhood. She encourages women to identify with her in order to discover their own divine qualities. In the *Candamaharosana Tantra*, a work that discusses the feminine roles and character, Vajrayogini explains how she is linked to all women and strongly defends the importance of womanhood for Buddhist enlightenment. She believes self-respect arises from deep within. Her strong and dynamic personality exemplifies feminine empowerment, showing that enlightened wisdom can be achieved in the human female body in this life.

Sometimes Vajrayogini manifests herself as an ugly old crone. The famous patriarch of the Kagyu sect, Naropa, had an encounter with Vajrayogini that changed his life. According to the legend, Naropa was sitting with his back to the sun, studying his books. Suddenly, a dark, ominous-looking shadow fell over him. He turned to look behind him and saw a hideous old woman who, unknown to him, was Vajrayogini. She asked him, "What are you studying?"

He answered, "I am studying grammar, philosophy, logic, and spiritual precepts."

She asked, "Do you understand the words or the sense of the words?"

He said, "I understand the words."

She cheered loudly, dancing and screaming happily. Naropa, thinking he could please her even more, added, "And I understand the sense, too!"

Instantly her entire demeanor changed. She began crying and screaming. Naropa was baffled. "Why," he asked, "are you so miserable all of a sudden?"

She answered, "I was ecstatic that a great scholar like you was honest enough to admit that he only understood the words. But when you claimed to understand the sense, I knew you, too, were a fraud."

Realizing the truth in what she said, he expressed his sincere desire to delve deeper in his studies. She advised him to study with her brother, who understood both the words and their most profound sense, and then she vanished like a rainbow.

In this encounter, Vajrayogini shocked Naropa out of his everyday frame of reference with her eccentric behavior. Shock and surprise temporarily stop the flow of everyday thinking. This momentary gap offers an opening, and thereby a creative opportunity to learn something new, to fill it, to complete the pattern. Our hypnosis teacher, Milton H. Erickson, M.D., often used shock and surprise to help his patients break through stubborn patterns, to allow new, positive, and more adaptive reactions an opportunity to emerge. Throughout Tibetan literature, dakinis often behaved erratically, challenging assumptions, often confusing and surprising the people they taught. These strange antics are actually effective methods that help students grow.

Balance of Masculine and Feminine

Dakinis also represent the female qualities of all people, the feminine side in the male-female unity. Both the masculine and feminine are viewed as two sides of the psyche and should be embraced. This is practiced within the mind of the practitioner.

We all have masculine and feminine qualities in our personalities. When a woman stands up to adversity she is expressing her masculine side. When a man shows tenderness to a young child he is expressing his feminine side. These behaviors are normal. Only when we are comfortable with both aspects of ourselves do we fully express our humanity. As Carl Jung pointed out,

> We can safely assert that these syzygies [male-female sides] are as universal as the existence of man and women. From this fact we may reasonably conclude that man's imagination is bound by this motif, so that he was largely compelled to project it again and again, at all times and in all places. (Jung 1980, 59–60)

Tibetan literature pictures male deities with their female counterparts, always in pairs. These images are symbolic of an individual's own thought content, recognizing this interplay within each person. We should come to terms with these opposing forces in ourselves and find their perfect union in enlightenment.

Tibetan Buddhist practices help people to accept both sides of themselves and allow these elements to come into balance. "Dakini is the necessary compliment to render us (whether male or female) whole beings" (Willis 1995, 73).

MALE-FEMALE RELATIONSHIPS

Both the male and female are important for reaching enlightenment. Dakinis are the necessary compliment to males. "She is what is lacking, the lacking of what prevents our complete enlightenment" (Willis 1995, 73).

Since both the masculine and feminine are important poles in the unity, through a mutually respectful and intimate relationship a deeper understanding can be reached by men and women as a couple, together. "What is sought in the yoga of union is a quality of relationship into which each partner enters fully in order that both may be liberated simultaneously" (Shaw 1994b, 22).

Tantric literature encourages men to work with women, enhancing each other, as an effective method for reaching enlightenment. Tibetan Buddhist men recognize that women have just as much to teach them as they, in their turn, have to teach. They embark on the path together.

Famous Partners

Many great Tibetan yogis—Naropa, Marpa, and Tilopa to name a few—practiced with a partner, often over their entire lifetime. One of the most famous partnerships was Yeshe Tsogyel and her partner Padmasambhava, one of the first Indian Buddhists to bring Tantric Buddhism to Tibet.

Many legends surround Tsogyel's birth and life. From her early years she felt a religious calling and wished to follow the Buddhist path to enlightenment. But at first she was not given the chance. She was so beautiful that many local kings fought with each other for her hand in marriage. Not only was she uninterested in a worldly marriage, but she felt deeply sorrowed by the hostility and fighting that took place on her behalf. The emperor heard of her great beauty and took her for his wife. Even though this stopped the fighting, Tsogyel still felt unfulfilled. The emperor happened to be interested in learning Buddhism and offered Tsogyel to Padmasambhava as a gift in exchange for learning.

Tsogyel was now free to pursue her Tantric Buddhist studies. Padmasambhava told her to seek a partner to experience the mysteries of tantra. She followed his suggestion and through these experiences, developed her understanding of pleasure combined with emptiness. When she returned to Padmasambhava, he could see that she had learned a great deal. He said to her:

> *O yogini who has mastered the Tantra. The human body is the body of the accomplishment of wisdom. And the gross bodies of men and women are equally suited. But if a woman has strong aspiration, she has higher potential. (Willis 1995, 17)*

Tsongyel's relationship with Padmasambhava became one of equals, both devoted to a religious life. They also became sexual partners, sharing in the experience of bodily pleasures as a pathway to deeper wisdom and understanding for both of them.

Tsogyel devoted her later life to helping the poor, the sick, and the miserable. As part of Tibetan Buddhist mythology, Tsogyel accomplished this by manifesting herself as various emanations. For example, to childless couples she appeared as a son or daughter, to men desiring women she appeared as an attractive girl. Wherever people were suffering, she appeared to them as the solution, to bring happiness.

CONCLUSION

Tibetan Buddhism takes an integrative perspective that includes all sides of emotion and personality. Each and every quality must be embraced for enlightenment. This means that our feelings and instincts matter, including both their masculine and feminine expression. Unlike other forms of Buddhism, tantric practices utilize emotions, sexual instincts, and passions along with the intellect as pathways to wisdom. Enlightenment takes place in this body, now. How can we be enlightened without being passionate, intelligent, sexual beings that we are?

CHAPTER 9

Birth, Death, and In-Between

If you constantly contemplate death, your mind will turn toward spiritual practice, your strength to practice will be renewed, and you'll see death as uniting yourself with absolute truth.
—Tibetan teaching

What is death? Western science thinks of it as a moment of flatline, a shutting down of the life processes. To some people, death symbolizes final rest and absolute peace. Tibetans, however, believe that this is a narrow, incorrect perspective. People who have been revived from death often report having profound experiences, such as seeing a white light or reviewing their life in a flash. Tibetans take this as evidence that consciousness continues after death. They have developed a science of death, exploring inner consciousness just as scientists explore the outer world.

Tibetans view birth, life, and death as an ongoing continuum. Life is a between—the time between birth and death. The cycle continues after death with a between period lasting from death to rebirth. This continuum is very real to Tibetans, and they offer an interesting argument to justify their position. Few of us have any memory of our birth. Yet we are all absolutely certain that we were born. Similarly few of us remember our rebirth. So why are we so certain that we have not been reborn? Just because we do not remember the time between death and rebirth is not proof that these periods do not exist.

Each period on the continuum is part of a spiritual journey. With the proper effort, people can move toward higher and higher evolution until the clear light of enlightenment is finally reached. This puts a stop to continual rebirths, lives, and deaths, and brings one into a final blissful eternal nirvana.

FACING DEATH

Tibetan Buddhism teaches that people can begin to master cyclical existence by developing the proper attitudes about death. One of the most famous works on this subject, *Great Exposition of the States of the Path to Enlightenment* (*Lam Rim chen mo*) was written by Tsong Kha Pa (1357–1419), the founder of the Gelukpa sect. His book explains how to achieve enlightenment. The section on how to face death is an excellent guide for today.

We are all certain that we will eventually die, but most of us try not to think about it. Yet increasing our awareness of inevitable death is crucial to helping us live well. When we remain fully aware that life is time-limited, our attitude changes. We appreciate each moment as it happens and make better use of the time we do have. As Tsong Kha Pa said: "Therefore, the prejudice that one will not die is the source of all trouble, and the antidote to that—the mindfulness of death—is the source of all that is marvelous" (Lopez 1997, 429).

Although we all know that we will die, we cannot be certain when it will happen. If you think about it, there are many possible causes that bring about death, but few that bring about life. All types of unexpected events can cut life short. Even life-promoting food and water, if contaminated, can be a life-threatening poison. We may have the best intentions to stay fit and healthy, but we cannot control all the variables. As Guru Nagarjuna said, "Your life dwells among the causes of death like a lamp standing in a strong breeze" (Lopez 1997, 437). Facing these realities can help us to value the life that we do have and make the most of it.

At the time of death, only spiritual development matters. Our money and possessions must be left behind. How we lived life is all that we can bring into the transition. With this understanding firmly in mind, we must seek to spiritually develop during our lifetime. Buddhism offers a way to cultivate this development, giving people what they will need to cope well with death. Tsong Kha Pa advises:

> *Hence think, "It will certainly happen that I must discard all the marvels of this world, and having discarded them, go to another world. Furthermore, that will happen today." Think about how, at that time, only religious practice will serve as a refuge, a protection, a defense. (Lopez 1997, 439)*

Meditate on these three points: we will die, we do not know when, and only spiritual development matters. Contemplate these ideas to try to fully understand what they mean. This will help set you on a realistic path that, if followed sincerely and wholeheartedly, will inevitably lead to enlightenment.

BARDO THODOL, THE TIBETAN BOOK OF THE DEAD

The Tibetan Book of the Dead, attributed to Padmasambhava, is one of the important texts in human history. It is a guide for people going through the dying process so they can find their way to a higher rebirth and eventually to nirvana.

Evans-Wentz pointed out that many early cultures had guides to dying—*Egyptian Book of the Dead* and the Greek mythology of Hades are two. The fact that many of the ideas overlap are an indication of certain universal truths about human existence. Robert Wicks, a modern author, believes that the book was actually written to help with living. He said, "It is more reasonable to interpret the text as directed more toward the living than toward the dead, and directed more toward psychological realities than toward metaphysical ones" (Wicks 1997, 486). We can look at it in both ways, as a guide to becoming the best we can be in life and beyond.

Tibet's book on dying, entitled the *Bardo Thodol,* translates as *The Great Book of Natural Liberation Through Understanding in the Between.* But Evans-Wentz popularized the name *The Tibetan Book of the Dead,* which is the title most people recognize today.

The *Bardo Thodol* pilots people through the period that happens after death. The course they take during the "between" depends on how they lived their lives and the choices they make after death, which influence each other.

Tibetans believe that consciousness falls away gradually, not all at once. A guru reads the *Bardo Thodol* to the deceased for up to forty-nine days, during which time the individual is open to becoming enlightened. By the forty-ninth day the death process is complete, and people will either have found enlightenment or be reborn. This intermediate state between death and rebirth through which the *Bardo Thodol* takes the deceased is called a *bardo.* There are three levels of bardo: Chikhai Bardo, Chonyid Bardo, and Sidpa Bardo. At any time, as people travel through these bardos, they may discover enlightenment, thereby stopping the continuous cycle of birth, death, and rebirth.

Chikhai Bardo, the Clear Light

The first reading of the book begins as the individual stops breathing. The words of the book are read close to the deceased's ear and repeated over and over. The guru addresses the deceased as "Nobly born" and implores the deceased to discover his or her highest nature.

Upon death, the individual is first faced with a brilliantly transparent, clear light, which is the radiance of his or her own pure mind. This clear light is the natural state of the mind, unmarred and undistracted by any lower instincts, thoughts, or feelings. The guru encourages the individual to face the light and stay with it. During the first hour after death, people who have meditated during their lifetime can become instantly enlightened, but this is quite unusual. If the clear light is not at first recognized, a second opportunity to face the clear light comes again, lasting as long as this bardo continues, up to four days.

The Chonyid Bardo of Peaceful and Wrathful Deities

Most people cannot face the brilliance of the clear light and thus enter the second bardo, Chonyid Bardo. In this bardo, sounds, lights, and images of both peaceful and wrathful deities are encountered. The *Bardo Thodol* repeatedly states that the things people encounter are merely manifestations of their own mind. The guru encourages the deceased not to be frightened, since even the most fearsome wrathful deity comes from the individual's own thinking. In a sense, people are confronting the best and worst in themselves. The book councils people to squarely face and come to terms with their faults, so that the natural clear buddha mind can be fully embraced without any interference.

For seven days, the peaceful deities are encountered, each symbolizing certain positive qualities of mind. In order to face these deities fully, the deceased is encouraged to transcend personal negative limitations. For example, on the first day in the Chonyid Bardo, people will see the deity Vairochana the Father, seed of all that is, with his female consort, bathed in an intense blue light. In order to open themselves to nirvana, people must recognize their own stupidity and give it up. Many people are lured by the softer white light that obscures the Path. They cannot face themselves without illusion and so they turn away.

The book encourages a therapeutic transformation, away from petty, small-minded emotions—anger, egoism, attachment, and jealousy—and toward higher, universal sentiments—love, compassion, and wisdom. Each day follows with another peaceful deity and efforts to let go of negative human qualities. The seventh day culminates in a rainbow of color with all the peaceful deities gathered together in the form of a mandala to try to draw the deceased toward enlightenment.

But the negative inclinations that were indulged during life have become karma that pulls people away from enlightenment. Their journey through the bardo takes them face-to-face with the wrathful deities from the eighth to fourteenth days. The book describes hideous beings with numerous heads, many arms and legs, a terrifying gaze, adorned in human skulls, drinking blood, and wielding frightening weapons. The guru reassures the deceased not to be afraid because even these fearsome beings are merely one's own thought-forms, and are to be embraced and accepted.

Learning to accept all of ourselves, even the aspects we do not like, is part of deep psychotherapy. When people stop fighting their bad qualities they take the first steps to being aware. Negative patterns dissolve and the individual discovers inner peace. One client we treated suffered from a dual personality, one she liked and the other she hated. The two sides were in battle with each other, tearing her apart from within. Through therapy, she learned to accept both sides of herself. She gained more inner control as the two sides became less extreme.

In the *Bardo Thodol*, the guru tells the deceased over and over that even the most frightening experience is just a mental image. If people realize this, they reach enlightenment.

Sidpa Bardo, The Path to Rebirth

Many people cannot believe that such fearful creatures could possibly come from their own thoughts, so they fight them, plummeting down into Sidpa Bardo, the third and most terrifying bardo. This bardo itself can last up to the final forty-ninth day of the process.

Because deceased people have no body, they must keep moving, yet they feel uncertain. "What should I do?" they ask. Throughout the journey at this level, individuals will experience extreme suffering and discomfort.

First they face judgment, similar to that in Western religions, where good deeds and bad deeds are counted and weighed. Through this process it is imperative to be absolutely honest. Self-deception will weigh negatively. The guru cautions the deceased to be careful what they think because impure thoughts lead downward. The book encourages people to think about the buddha, the dharma, and the sangha, to draw strength and guidance from them. If people remain focused, they can still become enlightened.

At this level, people are moving closer to their rebirth. Tibetan Buddhism sees six possible levels of rebirth, three positive (human, demi-god, god) and three negative (animal, hungry ghost, hellbeing). In the bardo, each of these has its own light that shines on the deceased, depending upon the kind of life he or she has led.

The book describes five methods to close the womb door and thereby avoid rebirth. Earnestness and faith are two ways. The third is reminiscent of Freud, the originator of psychoanalysis's oedipal complex. The *Bardo Thodol* states, exactly as Freud did, that males naturally feel hatred for their father and love for their mother. Females experience the reverse: love for their father and hate for their mother. If people can transcend these feelings and meditate on the symbolic mother/father figure as their teacher, they will find nirvana. The fourth method is to meditate on how everything we experience is illusory, and finally the fifth is to meditate on the clear light. If none of these methods are possible, the individual is reborn at one of the six levels. Thus the cycle begins again with the potential to eventually find liberation through enlightenment.

By gaining control over the mind, even the lowest, most depraved scoundrel can change for the better and become enlightened. In this way, the *Bardo Thodol* offers hope to all humanity, for even though we may be imperfect, we can achieve complete liberation and total bliss at any time during the continuum of existence.

CHAPTER 10

Enlightenment Brings Wisdom and Compassion

Remember, our purpose is not to make more Buddhists, it is to make more enlightened beings. When you teach Buddhism, don't encourage people to become Buddhists; just encourage them to cultivate the qualities of love, compassion, universal responsibility and wisdom within themselves.
—His Holiness the Dalai Lama

Some Western philosophers, such as Immanuel Kant, believed that we are forced by time and space to always have a limited perception of reality. By contrast, Buddhists are convinced that direct perception is not only possible but also inevitable if we allow ourselves to look using the proper methods. We can experience ultimate reality, and this experience is enlightenment. Through meditation, we transcend the limited perspective given to us by our senses and perceive the world as it truly is.

This view opens up a new set of assumptions, a different perspective with new possibilities. In the Kantian world of space and time only certain things are possible, but from the enlightened perspective, new potentials are everywhere. This has ramifications in many fields, such as opening new treatments for healing. According to Plotinus, the ancient Greek philosopher who was considered by Evans-Wentz to be the closest Western thinker to Tibetan Buddhism, human beings must live in both worlds of beliefs to attain their fullest potential.

Tibetan Buddhism offers a path to enlightenment. This path involves an inner transformation. Change begins within our own minds and brings about an intuitive understanding of the nature of the universe. Enlightenment brings great wisdom, but it also brings a deep feeling of compassion and caring for others. These two qualities of enlightenment—wisdom and compassion—bring satisfying happiness.

WISDOM OF ENLIGHTENMENT

Enlightened wisdom involves the understanding of emptiness. Emptiness is the realization that everything we know and experience is temporary. Nothing endures forever, and therefore everything is actually nonexistent in its inherent nature. When we contemplate in meditation, we experience this for ourselves. Just as thoughts come and go in our mind, so also material objects exist for a time and eventually deteriorate. Even our lives have time limits. Enlightened wisdom can see through the illusion of permanence that we give to our world, like looking beyond the horizon.

This idea can be understood if we think about virtual reality. Most people who use the Internet have seen that there is much to learn, do, and experience on-line. But everyone also knows that cyberspace is not reality—it is merely electromagnetic pulses. Yet we use it, do things with it, as it appears, and in this sense treat it as real. Similarly, the world we live in seems permanent, to be used and experienced. Yet ultimately, it is as fleeting and empty as cyberspace.

If things are empty, then what are they? When we search for the true nature of things, we discover nothing is there. Even when we look for the thinker who thinks about where the thinker is, we find no one and nothing. Ultimately all is empty. Emptiness is the true nature of reality. The intuitive realization of this, discovered by meditation, brings a blissful feeling of enlightenment.

COMPASSION

Enlightened wisdom also shows us that we are not alone in the world. In fact, we are all made of the same nonstuff, emptiness, and in this way we are all united. Thus, wisdom shows us that the true way to be in accord with enlightenment is to be compassionate. Tibetan Buddhists have developed ways to enhance our feelings of compassion so that it becomes a natural expression of living.

Enlightened compassion is love for all beings in the world. Enlightened love differs from worldly love in that enlightened people make no distinction: They love all beings alike. In worldly love, we have stronger feelings for the individuals who are in our close circle, and we feel indifference or even dislike for people who are distant. Buddhism teaches people to love everyone equally and to express that love as compassion and caring for the world as a whole.

ENLIGHTENMENT IN THIS LIFE NOW

The wisdom and compassion of enlightenment lead to a way of living that is an expression of that wisdom and compassion. Tibetan Buddhism encourages people to develop wisdom and compassion so that they can live enlightened lives, which means immersing themselves fully in life. Everything matters. This life here and now is where enlightenment is discovered. Ultimate reality is not beyond everyday reality: they are one and the same.

Everything around you can serve as a symbol of enlightenment, to be used as an opportunity to deepen your understanding, as this story illustrates. An accomplished monk moved out of the monastery. One day a fellow student saw him shoveling dirt at a construction site. Shocked to see such a respected monk engaged in a lowly activity he asked him, "What are you doing here?"

The monk answered, "With every pile of dirt I move I am removing illusion from my mind. The dirt is my teacher."

Each action, experience, relationship—everything in our lives—is symbolic of enlightened insight. The more you experience, feel, and think, the more closely immersed you become in enlightenment. You should not try to escape from your life to become wise. Everyday life is sacred, and every action is a ritual on the path. Enlightenment is discovered through living your life in this way. Living with wisdom and compassion makes it all worthwhile.

The relationships and circumstances of life should not be avoided, but rather embraced as the ground within which enlightened consciousness comes to be experienced. If this world of samsara *is* nirvana, we should not avoid our lives, regardless of whether we have fortune, success, and good relationships, or misfortune, poverty, and interpersonal conflict. Each situation has something to teach, an aspect of enlightenment to experience, if comprehended with the correct mind-set. As the Dalai Lama explained, anger can be overcome by realizing that even enemies bring opportunities to become wiser and more compassionate. We evolve through interaction. Important insight is gained from difficult situations. We can appreciate these negative experiences and people because no positive experience could ever give us the same opportunity to transcend and grow. When we face hostility with patience, for example, we gain perseverance, while the people who lose their tempers become diminished. Any apparent outer gains they might seem to receive are unreal and deceptive, for in terms of their inner world, they have taken a step backward.

Tibetan Buddhists believe that we should utilize all the qualities given to us as resources on our Path. Our capacity to think and feel should not be blunted, but should be sharpened as useful tools. Even interpersonal relationships can be helpful. In the shared experience of intimacy, enlightenment can be found for both people together. As Atisa taught, we can develop an adamantine steadfastness to maintain meditative awareness and do the right thing even in the midst of deep feelings. In this ability to stay on the enlightened course in every situation, people discover complete happiness and blissful joy.

Life becomes the expression of enlightenment. In Hindu literature, the point of enlightenment is when the dewdrop of the individual's mind merges with the ocean of universal mind. But in Tibetan Buddhism, enlightenment is when the ocean of universal mind is permitted to express itself through the individual mind—an apparent reversal, due to understanding that the individual mind is only a relative, temporary illusory experience. Every action, every thought, every feeling is enlightenment. This enlightened expression functions as a skillful means to guide others to find enlightenment as well.

SEEKING THE ENLIGHTENED PATH

Tibetans like to look at the Buddhist journey as a continuum: birth, life, death, rebirth; and so the cycle continues until final enlightenment for all beings is reached. The tantric path is always in flux, but it can be broken down into stages, somewhat similar to how the high school years are broken down into grades: sophomore, junior, senior.

The first step is to recognize that we can become enlightened if we really want to. We all have the power to guide ourselves away from the negative and toward the positive, and this is how it begins. The laws of karmic evolution show that positive and negative deeds plant seeds that bear certain fruits: positive actions produce future happiness while negative actions bring future misery. When you meditate on the understanding that negative actions will only bring you unhappiness, you find it easier to abandon killing, stealing, inappropriate sexual activity, lying, speaking harshly, slandering others, gossiping, covetous thoughts, or having ill will.

Think about what would happen if you did perform an evil act—for example, someone who is violent plants the seeds for further violence. The environment that such individuals create becomes uncomfortably hostile. Their lives are filled with turmoil and misery. If you want your life to be happy, violence should be abandoned. The change process involves becoming aware of shortcomings, developing remorse about them, and attempting to avoid such actions in the future.

Once you start living more in accord with the positive, you can begin to extend your understanding toward enlightened wisdom. This involves practicing meditation that teaches how to maintain awareness and keep thoughts clear and focused. During this phase, as you begin to glimpse the joys and satisfactions of enlightenment, motivation raises even further. You may have experienced this natural motivation in small ways when, for example, you saw a preview for a movie you want to see or read a review of a book you find interesting. You find yourself wanting very much to experience it for yourself, and may not stop thinking about it until you have seen the movie or read the book.

The third phase is the highest expression of Buddhism: generating the spirit of compassion. Once people have experienced a glimpse of enlightenment, they naturally want to help others. "The Seven-Point Oral Tradition of Cause and Effect" teaches how to develop a compassionate attitude that is motivated from within, not from someone outside telling you to do it. This series of meditations shows step by step how to extend the natural loving feelings we all have for mothers to all people in the world (see Chapter 15 for the instructions).

Just developing the mind of a bodhisattva is not enough. You also need to train in the activities of a bodhisattva using the six perfections—generosity, ethical discipline, patience, perseverance, concentration, and wisdom—to improve yourself. Thus, to improve your generosity, practitioners are encouraged to "cut the knot of miserliness constricting the heart" (Mullin 1982, 151). They begin with little things—sharing bits of food with a wild bird, for example—until, eventually, every action they do is generous. Instructions are given for each perfection to help bring about a transformation, not simply of thought but also of action.

The highest and most intensive training at this level is the Vajrayana. This requires initiation and practice with a guru. The guru guides the practitioner, pointing out what to seek and what to avoid. Practitioners can realize the continuum and intertwine all the understandings together through meditative concentration and penetrative insight. Even amid adversity, enlightenment is here and now. Nothing can deter the adamantine spirit of these bodhisattvas from the Path. They visualize themselves as highly evolved using Deity Yoga tantras, and eventually, become wise and compassionate beings who unconditionally devote themselves to helping the world.

YOUR ENLIGHTENMENT

Enlightenment begins as you change your way of living. By giving up the negative and turning toward the positive, transformation subtly takes place. Meditation brings about new perspectives—a change in consciousness. You no longer feel the same way about life. You can recognize the interconnections between all people, you feel your Oneness with the universe. You have entered the mandala and can share in the wisdom of all the buddhas.

PART III

Living Tibetan Buddhism

Symbols surround us
Show us the One
Enter the circle
Transform and become
—C. Alexander Simpkins

Tibetan Buddhism opens the doorway of your mind to new ways of experiencing your life. Free your potential as you enter the circle of the mandala. Part III shows how to adapt these tantric methods to your own life so that you can transform within—and fulfill your potential with wisdom and compassion.

CHAPTER 11

Meditating the Tantric Way

Do not imagine, do not think, do not analyze, do not meditate, do not reflect; Keep the mind in its natural state.
—Tilopa

Tibetan Buddhism has a rich tradition of tantric meditation that incorporates all aspects of the human mind and body. Every capacity you have can be developed. Through meditation, you can hone and refine yourself to live life fully and become the best person you can be.

Tantric meditation uses many of the abilities that are natural to us as human beings. We can use our capacity to imagine, to visualize, to feel our emotions, and to move our bodies. Everything you are becomes symbolic of your inner transformation.

Approach these meditation skills in the same way you would learn a new sport or a musical instrument: by carefully following the instructions and practicing persistently. This chapter offers a number of ways to train yourself in tantric methods of meditation. Use these methods in the later chapters as you continue your journey to inner development.

READYING FOR MEDITATION

To perform meditation for the first time, find a quiet place where you can be undisturbed for a little while. You may begin with as little as five minutes and increase the duration with practice.

Traditionally, meditation has been performed sitting on a small pillow on the floor. If sitting cross-legged on the floor is comfortable for you, then follow the tradition. However, do not let sitting on the floor become a hurdle. When we teach meditation classes, we often have several students who, for one reason or another, cannot sit comfortably on the floor. We encourage them to sit in a chair. What is most important for meditation is simply that you do it, not how or where you sit. Find what is comfortable for you.

The traditional posture for meditation is cross-legged or in a half-lotus position, where one foot rests on top of the opposite leg. Allow your back to be relatively straight so that your breathing passages are free and open. Try not to strain. Rest your hands on your lap. Tibetan Buddhism has certain hand postures, called *mudras*, which we will use later in the chapter. At first, simply find a position for your hands that feels comfortable.

Now, with an open mind, you are ready to experience meditation and all the benefits it can bring.

MAHAMUDRA: THE GREAT SYMBOL

According to Evans-Wentz, the meditation instructions of the Mahamudra are one of the greatest gifts we have received from the East. He said, "It contains the quintessence of some of the most profound doctrines of Oriental Occultism" (Evans-Wentz 1967, 101).

Mahamudra is not just a set of techniques but a point of view. Working much like a microscope, these methods help the practitioner focus the lens of mental perception on deeper levels of reality. When you look at a skin cell through a microscope at a low power of magnification, you see a great many details. But magnify to a high power and a whole other world of tiny cells and membranes opens up to you. Use the greater magnification of an electron microscope, and the form and structure of the world as we know it completely disappears. Boundaries are no longer evident. We see an infinitesimal reality of electrons and neutrons—pure energy. Similarly, the Mahamudra trains perception to see beyond the illusory world our senses reveal, showing us the deeper nature of reality: empty of substance, pure energy. With the clear eye of Mahamudra, the world jumps out in clarity, like when you first leave a dark movie theater after a matinee and the world seems brighter, more vivid. By removing all illusions, what remains is extraordinary vividness.

The meditations that follow are drawn from the larger body of instructions. If you would like to pursue this method in greater depth, we encourage you to find a knowledgeable guru who can guide you on your Path. These exercises will lead you to one-pointed awareness, an ability that can become your tool for mental focus and inner discipline to be carried with you in everything you do.

Outer One-Pointed Awareness

This ancient yogic practice begins by teaching you how to focus your mind on one thing. Take a small ball or piece of wood and place it in front of you. Look at it intently as you focus all your attention only on this object. Think only of this object. If you notice your thoughts wandering, gently bring them back to this object. With repeated practice you will find that your thoughts quiet and your attention becomes more focused.

Inner One-Pointed Awareness

This exercise focuses attention on breathing. Close your eyes and count each complete breath, in and out. The ancient texts had people count to

21,600 breaths! You can begin by counting to ten and then repeating. Begin with several minutes and lengthen the time to what feels comfortable for you.

As your concentration on counting the breaths improves, focus your attention on breathing itself. Notice the air as it comes in through your nose and travels down into your lungs. Pay close attention to how long it is restrained until you exhale. Gradually you will become well acquainted with the breathing process and develop your ability to remain focused.

Now that you have begun to discipline your mental processes, you can develop a meditative attitude.

Taming Thought by Letting Be

In this meditation, turn your one-pointed focus inward to observe your own thinking. Pay close attention to the appearance and disappearance of your thoughts, but do not try to stop them or control them in any way. Simply allow yourself to observe the process. Don't follow any particular thoughts, but don't impede them either. Simply notice as you keep yourself detached from the thoughts.

Eventually, you will become calmer. You will have moments without thoughts. Your attention becomes like that of a young child who is intensely mentally alert looking at something fascinating. At the same time, like an elephant that is indifferent to the prick of a thorn, nothing need distract you.

Calmness of an Ocean Without a Wave

Buddhism teaches that the thinker and the thought are One. You can experience this for yourself with meditation. Perform the previous exercise again and notice how your thoughts are continually in motion as you refrain from being carried away with any one thought. Keep your mind at rest. As you continue to meditate in this way, you will experience a falling away of any separation between the motion of your arising thoughts and the rest of your clear, observing mind. This is the realization of one-pointed awareness.

VISUALIZATION MEDITATIONS

Once you gain the skills of one-pointed awareness, you can use it to perceive the deeper nature of yourself and your life. You can turn your awareness to anything in your environment. Every situation can become a symbol of transformation. These methods use both mind and body, motion and stillness. The meditations that follow introduce you to the tantric methods of meditation.

Tibetan Buddhism uses visualizations in many meditations. Some people are natural visualizers—they picture things automatically, remember things vividly. For others, visualizing is more challenging. You can learn how to visualize with practice. Do these exercises, step by step, and you will improve over time.

Visualization I

If you have had difficulty visualizing, this exercise will help give you a definite experience of visualization, since it is based on the way the visual receptors of the eye function. Take a bright red piece of colored paper and tape it to a white wall. Stand several feet back and look at the red square for two minutes. Then, close your eyes. You will see a green square appear in your visual field.

Visualization II

At a later time, close your eyes. Try to recall the red square that you placed on the wall. Then think about the green image you saw. Let your imagination play with these two images. Can you picture red more easily than green, or vice versa? Practice visualizing one of these colors when you close your eyes.

Visualization III

Write the letters *OM* on a standard sheet of paper, filling most of the page. Trace the letters with your finger, moving from left to right, for several minutes. Keep tracing and looking at the letters. Repeat this exercise several times a day for two days. On the third day, look briefly at the paper and then close your eyes and try to visualize the whole image in your mind. Repeat this exercise until you can hold the entire image in your mind.

BODY MEDITATIONS

Tantric Buddhism recognizes that truth resides within our bodies. We can discover enlightenment in the human body when we properly turn our attention to it. Tantric meditations use the mind's one-pointed awareness combined with mudras and mantras. The following meditations are samples.

Mantra Meditation

The sound of your voice can become the focus of meditation. Chant the mantra HUM AH OM. Repeat the sounds, over and over. Keep your mind focused on the sound and the vibrations.

Breathing Visualization

You can use your visualization to unify breathing with awareness. Visualize that each inhalation is the syllable HUM and blue in color. Picture the moment of retention of the breath as the syllable AH, red in color. Finally, visualize the expiration of air as the syllable OM and white. Repeat the process until it becomes natural.

Integrative Meditation: Mantra, Mudra, and Visualization

Sit cross-legged with your hands resting palms down on your knees. Imagine HUM as your breath is taken in. Pause after you have taken in your breath. This pause between inhale and exhale is a momentary glimpse at emptiness. Bring your fingertips up to the center of your chest as you hear the syllable AH in your mind. Now exhale with the sound OM in your mind as you move your hands to rest palms up on your knees. Repeat the pattern for a few minutes at first, increasing to twenty minutes.

Body Warming

Tummo is the ability to generate psychic body heat. Tibetan Buddhists learn how to visualize so vividly that their bodies act like human batteries, generating heat. These skills are tested. Practitioners must sit outside on an icy night. A wet sheet is placed directly on the meditator's bare back. Through the power of concentration he generates enough body heat to dry the sheet. Accomplished practitioners can dry many sheets, one after the other.

These practitioners show us that body temperature can be controlled by the mind. The procedures used in Tummo are very complex, but you can experiment with this exercise to help begin to free yourself from the constraints of temperature.

Sit quietly for a moment. Begin by testing the temperature of your palm. Touch your palm to your upper arm. Notice how warm or cool your palm feels. Now, place your two palms together, fingers pointing outward from your lap. Close your eyes. Visualize warmth arising between your hands. You could visualize a fire in a fireplace, warmth from the sun, or even a space heater. Use an image that is vivid in your experience. Imagine the warmth spreading up your arms. When you are ready to stop, test your palm temperature again and compare it to how warm it felt when you started. With practice, you will be able to feel a difference.

Tibetan Monks creating a sand mandala, October–November 1999,
Mesa College, San Diego, California.

CHAPTER 12

Entering Through Art

If art is evocative, then the artists of Tibet manifest an evocative power that is astonishing both in the breadth of vision and its artistic realization.
—Pratapaditya Pal, *The Art of Tibet*

We have a long tradition in the West of assuming that abstraction is a step away from the central reality, that the concrete, what we can point to, is more fundamental. We attempt to get in touch and speak of getting back to basics, to ground level. We perceive in terms of unity, and consider the whole, the pattern, to be natural. This is due to the natural tendency to complete a form, to make it whole: closure, the good form. But there is another way to perceive reality.

In experimental situations, psychologists have noticed that when people continue to look at a well-defined pattern long enough, it begins to deconstruct into abstractions of simpler parts.

Deconstructing Exercise

Stare at an object you know well—a statue or a vase—for twenty minutes or so. Eventually you will no longer perceive it as a stable, complex form. The parts will no longer be united in the same complex pattern as the original object. Your perceptual processes will automatically alter your experience of the object into simpler forms. Observe how the lines change, the angles and tones. Note the thoughts that occur to you.

The mind naturally tends to abstract. We need change, variation. Therefore, abstraction is not just getting away from what is real. It is actually a return to basics. Simple lines and patterns are fundamental to our perception of reality. They express something deeper.

Tibetan Buddhism uses this natural tendency towards abstraction in art to help practitioners get in touch with important concepts and insights. The mandala, with its simple form, the circle, is one of these ways. Artifacts, paintings, and prayer flags are other examples. Tibetan art offers a glimpse of higher realities through form, which shows relationships and principles.

Just as the visionary artist shows us a view of the universe that he is able to see with his imagination, Tibetan Buddhism opens possibilities of perception to us. This is the valuable use of arts for society. Art can show us a different perspective and give us a way to comprehend some aspect of our reality, to derive meaning. Art is integral to this philosophy. Vision becomes reality.

IMAGERY

The soul never thinks without an image. (Aristotle in Arnheim 1969, 12)

Psychologists are finding that intelligence is not just a matter of reason. Our ability to understand is often the result of our highly sophisticated visual system, which has an intelligence all its own. We often understand images better than words. Pictures and diagrams can be very useful to communicate ideas. For example, directions to a place are often better understood when a map is drawn than when a description is given.

Visual imagery talent is sometimes present along with verbal talent, and sometimes not. We all know people who can draw or sketch an idea better than explain it in words.

Visual imagery is useful for learning and remembering. An idea can be memorized more easily, often, when we can think of it as a picture. Mnemonic memory systems rely on this. To remember names or a date, try to associate it with an image of some kind. (See our book *Living Meditation* for a number of exercises applying this.)

Experiments have shown that people can usually remember sets of pictures better than sets of words. In one experiment by Lionel Standing, groups of subjects were shown 10,000 pictures over a five-day period, then given a test that asked them to recognize them. He estimated that they could recall the general features of about 6,600 pictures! Another group was shown 1,000 pictures with unusual details, 1,000 ordinary pictures, and 1,000 words. In comparison, subjects could recall and recognize differences between 880 vivid pictures, 770 ordinary pictures, but only 615 words. Their memory for words was not as good as their memory for images (Standing 1973, 207–222).

Allan Paivio, a renowned Canadian researcher in cognitive psychology, developed a theory of dual coding to enhance memory (Reed 1996, 183). He was able to demonstrate experimentally that words and images could work together to give alternate codes to use to remember something that is learned. If a word is forgotten, a picture or image associated with it could bring the idea to mind.

In order to recall a speech, a classic ancient text for giving speeches on mnemonic memory known as *Ad Herennium*, written 86–82 B.C., author unknown, suggests that topics of a speech can best be remembered by translating them into images. Imagine walking through a building with a place and room for each idea to remind yourself of the concepts and other parts of the speech. By entering the mandala, the student gains insight from the gurus. The founders' concepts are stored and represented there in signs and symbols, as images. Tibetan Buddhism evolves this further. The student becomes one with the principles and meaning and, ultimately, the new perception. This would naturally be expected, since there is no separation, no boundary possible. Buddha and the images of Buddha are one, and equally illusory. The image helps to show the way to enlightenment.

Tibetan art can be used to transcend limitations of comprehension, to communicate meanings, and to learn the relationships of ideas. Mandalas, statues, and artifacts encode the wisdom of the past and also reveal insight as experience. Finally, they may reveal new interpretations, as in the terma of the Nyingmas.

ART REFLECTIONS OF MIND

Tibetan Buddhist art expresses the philosophy in exquisite detail. In murals, thangkas (banners), paintings, and sculptures we see before us the array of buddhas, bodhisattvas, and deities. When viewing a beautiful goddess or a frightening demon, keep in mind the advice from the *Tibetan Book of the Dead*: All of the colorful characters pictured in Tibetan art are symbolic of the inner mind. You can feel reflections of deeper, more archaic thoughts and feelings. For example, a fierce and fiery image of a wrathful deity might represent archaic feelings of anger or frustration. A statue of a sensual dakini reflects sexuality or sensitivity. To look at Tibetan art is to turn your attention back to archaic emotions and images, to explore your inner world through experience. Let the outer reveal the inner as you step through Alice's looking glass into the world of the mandala. Travel deeper and deeper until you come face-to-face with the center—your inner core—one with all humanity and at ease with who you are, so you can evolve to develop your most positive potentials.

TRADITIONAL FORMS OF ART

Sculptures in Tibet were most commonly done in metal, clay, and stucco, and statues often represented deities in Tibetan Buddhist literature. Typically, statues take a dynamic pose, capturing movement in a flash. Sharp angles of arms and legs, often with a strong diagonal composition, dramatize the power and energy of these images. These sculptures dramatize the dynamic energy and richness of the inner spirit.

Two-dimensional art was done as murals on the walls of temples and as prints on tapestries and banners. Many paintings portray the whole of Tibetan Buddhist philosophy as a single, complex image, filled with details. Typical, for example, are mandalas created in intricate detail. Figures are dressed in decorative costumes rich in colors: reds, greens, browns, and gold. Intended to help practitioners look within themselves, the mandala shows the entire universe, pictured as the mind of the meditator. "As a picture, the thangka opens up vistas for him, but it presents also, in a preliminary form, the experience of vision" (Pal 1969, 38).

Tibetan monks have also created mandalas in sand. The work is done using different colors of sand, beginning at the center and moving outward. The sand is carefully and accurately sprayed into place using harmonics to gently vibrate the grains of sand. After the mandala is completed and shown for a short time, these masterpieces are thrown into a river or sea in accord with the impermanence of life.

Rather than representing the outer world, Tibetan art renders the inner vision, and in so doing opens this possibility for the viewer: to look at the world as a symbol of inner experience in all the richness and depth that the human mind is capable of experiencing. As Milarepa so aptly put it: "That all the wealth revealed within my mind, and all the circling threefold worlds contain, Unreal as it is, can yet be seen—that is the miracle" (Milarepa in Pal 1969, 13).

The art represents dharma teachings, just as life itself can symbolize Buddhist wisdom. Each deity is pictured holding characteristic objects with mudras to symbolize their particular areas of understanding. For example, Manjushri, the god of wisdom, is often pictured with a sword in his hand to symbolize his severance of emotional attachments. Everything can be interpreted as a manifestation of enlightenment.

TRAINING TO TRANSCEND

In the 1960s, experiments in hypnosis were conducted by Russian researcher Vladimir Raikov. Using hypnotic trance, he suggested to his subjects that they become the reincarnation of a certain great painter, a great sculptor, etc., for one week, each character, and during that time to create as that painter or sculptor would. At the end of the period of training, they were awakened, with no conscious memory of the experience, and asked to create as themselves. Raikov reported a dramatic change in the abilities of some of the subjects—some of the skills gained through the role-playing were somehow absorbed. Perhaps they discovered unrecognized potentials of their own.

The principle behind this may be similar to Deity Yoga. Each of us has great untapped potential within, and we may glimpse this potential as our ideals and positive fantasies, even by our representations of what is possible only for others. But we are also the other, not just ourselves. Deity Yoga may tap into similar mental mechanisms. Imagining themselves as a buddha, practitioners may realize and absorb some of the positive qualities. Of course, in everyday reality, they are not literally the deity, but the deity can represent their best qualities. To activate these positive potentials, to become the best person you can be, to the Tibetan Buddhist, means to become a buddha.

Art moves beyond merely being a symbolic representation. The form of Tibetan painting with a meditator at the center may be taken to literally express the philosophical method of Deity Yoga. The center can be seen as the meditating clear mind, invoking deities to help, pictured as the surrounding figures. The Tibetans believe that the artistic rendering of a buddha can literally embody the presence of the Buddha himself. A central idea in all of Buddhism is that no one is different from Buddha. Only our deluded thinking prevents us from recognizing our true nature. Visualization is the method to reawaken this in ourselves, by clearly picturing an image of Buddha as the true Buddha with all of the wonderful qualities he possesses. The next step is to identify with and take these qualities into yourself—to become as wise and compassionate as it is possible to be, until you are a buddha in your own right.

VISUALIZING A MANDALA

Visualization skills are used on the path to exploring Buddhism. As was discussed in Chapter 7, the mandala, based on the circle, is a symbolic representation of deeper reality. Skilled practitioners learn to visualize complex mandalas down to the most minute detail and hold the entire image, with all its intricate detail, in their minds all at once. You can begin to build these skills by starting simply. Eventually you will be able to hold more complex patterns in your mind, not only enhancing your meditation abilities but also improving your memory and learning capacities.

Practice the visualization meditations in Chapter 11. Once you feel comfortable with simple visualizations, try this classic Tibetan Buddhist exercise.

Mandala Meditation

Look at one of the mandalas pictured in this book. Observe carefully, noticing everything about it. After you feel that you know it fairly well, close your eyes and try to hold this mental image in your mind. If you have gaps, open your eyes and look. Then close your eyes and try again. Work with this until you can visualize the mandala fairly accurately and keep the image in your mind. Practice this repeatedly as this skill will be useful for later meditations.

Visualizing Your Mandala

Sit in meditation, eyes closed, mind relaxed. Experience yourself in the center of your own mandala, meditating. Then, reach out with your imagination to those people and places closest to you, perhaps your home, your family, your closest friends. Then picture people and places that are farther away but still important in your world. Keep ranging out as far as you can until you feel that your mandala is complete. You might visualize them in place, like the traditional art pieces, or simply keep the picture purely intuitive. Allow yourself to feel that you are not alone, but always a part of this greater whole.

Creating Your Own Mandala

The mandalas to be found in monasteries and temples are of no particular significance because they are external representations only. The true mandala is always an inner image, which is gradually built up through (active) imagination. (Jung 1981, 170)

Gather the materials you will need to create your own mandala. You can use crayons, chalk, pens, pencils, computer, or even sand—whatever medium flows best for you. When you have everything ready, sit quietly in meditation. Develop your focused, one-pointed awareness and then begin. As you work, focus your mind on your inner experience. You can make it as detailed or simple as you choose, using symbols that are meaningful to you. We have included a samples of a personal mandala. Let yourself be creative. May you grow with the experience.

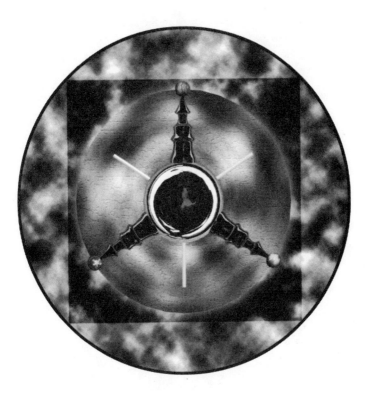

**Meditative Universe, Contemporary mandala, August 2000,
C. Alexander Simpkins Jr., San Diego, California.**

CHAPTER 13

Martial Arts:
Enlightened Patterns

Look for that which is not easily seen.
—Bubishi

You can adapt methods and principles from Tibetan Buddhist philosophy to enhance your skills in your martial art. These principles can also be applied to any physical activity that you do.

ENTER THE MANDALA THROUGH FORMS

Many martial artists practice forms as a way to perfect technique and learn their art. Forms are the literature of the style, patterns that express the movements and strategies used. Students learn different forms at each level of proficiency. The exercises that follow can help to enhance your learning and performance of forms.

Mandala Pattern Exercise

The pattern of the form or technique in martial arts should be vividly imagined. Try to make it real, as if three-dimensional. Consider the directions as lines of force, pushing and pulling in the directions of movement, weaving you together with your opponent.

Find the center of the form or technique, and move outward from there. For example, white belts performing their first form will need to focus all their attention on simple body positioning in order to perform their basic blocks, kicks, and strikes correctly. This is the meaning, the center of the form for them at this level, but as the practitioner evolves, the center changes. An advanced practitioner performing a white belt form will try to express accuracy, flow, power, and other important ideals of the style.

This method can be applied to other intensely involving physical activities with a clear form or pattern. Moving in distinct patterns has long been a part of culture, expressed as rituals and customs. For example, folk dancing utilizes the patterns for a different purpose, such as having fun while expressing cultural meanings. Dancers express mood, emotions, even a story in their performances. A dancer can enhance the quality of movement by meditating on the fundamental patterns and what they express.

Enter the Form Exercise

Observe the form or pattern as the master intends it to be expressed. As you observe, do you sense a certain spirit within the form, does it have a feeling and rhythm? In kung fu arts, especially the animal styles, the spirit within the form evolved from a deep understanding of the animal itself. When the spirit of the form and the practitioner unite in performance, a mysterious transformation takes place. Movements take on a subtly different quality: if a tiger, we see great power and ferocity; if a crane, we feel its evasive, graceful flow; if a lion, we hear its roar.

Do not try to think of how you should behave during the execution of the form. Just do it, imagine the feeling, the spirit, and enter into it.

MANTRAS OF MARTIAL ARTS: THE YELL

Mantras are chanted to enhance the focus of consciousness and create a mental condition conducive to inner concentration. Martial arts also use sounds to help focus mind, body, and spirit together in a single moment. Any technique can be affected positively by articulating sounds. The practitioner utters sounds while going through motions: breathing with loud exhales and yells are a part of intense committed practice. These sounds are like the mantras of Buddhism. More power can be generated when personally inspiring sounds are made. A loud "utz!," "yaah!," or "kyap!" may help practitioners raise and focus their energy to break wood or bricks with ease. The sound, the force of the technique, and the break should happen simultaneously.

Mantra Exercise

Some students have trouble letting out a yell. Others do not use it to its greatest advantage, as a meditative tool for mental focus. First clear your mind of distractions. Then, practice your technique adding a yell. Perform the two simultaneously. Allow your yell to come from deep down as you exhale. Put your effort into the performance of the technique/yell. Do not hold back. Repeat until you can perform fully with focused spirit.

MANAGING ANGER

Another important application of this philosophy can be used when applying techniques in sparring. Sometimes practitioners find that if the opponent scores a point or attacks hard, they feel their emotions rising. Before long, they have lost their concentration and the match. Adopting the Buddhist approach, your opponent can also be your teacher. The Dalai Lama has urged everyone to suspend anger. Maintain your composure. Then you will have the mental sharpness to respond to each situation with the best solution. During sparring, you have many opportunities to respond with calm and to cope well. Mistakes can be springboards to create new and better techniques to solve problems posed by your opponent. You learn and grow from your interaction, even if you lose a point, for the moment, to the opponent. You can appreciate a good point, whoever delivers it—though you may wish it were you.

Exercise in Anger Management

Sit quietly in meditation to clear your mind of distracting thoughts. When you are ready, imagine and review a sparring match or perhaps a time during class when you became annoyed by something that was done to you. Consider the principle that there is something positive to learn from this situation. For example, if the opponent scored on you, what was wrong with your defense? Think carefully. How can you improve as a result of this experience? As you contemplate, searching for answers, does your anger diminish? Can you become calmer as you appreciate your learning?

We can analyze the dynamics of our ways of weaving together to discern continuities, timeless fundamental patterns expressed in relationships. You can apply this to every aspect of your life. Think about the deeper patterns. In sport tournaments, self-defense, and the art within martial art, deeper understandings transcend the boundaries of the school, even of martial arts themselves. By getting in touch with fundamentals, an opportunity for higher insight is given.

CHAPTER 14

Dialogue with Science

We dance 'round in a ring and suppose
But the Secret sits in the middle and knows.
—Robert Frost

SCIENCE AND TIBETAN BUDDHISM

Science and Tibetan Buddhism ask similar questions: What is the nature of the universe? How can we best benefit humanity, now and in the future? Western science and technology have attempted to answer these questions by turning toward the material world. Tibetan Buddhism looks for answers following the spiritual path. The Dalai Lama has taken an active interest in science, in the belief that science and spirituality should walk hand in hand. He has actively engaged in a number of dialogues with scientists doing research in the areas of physics, neuroscience, and cognitive psychology. Despite some profound differences, there were also some areas of agreement. When such different methodologies lead to the same conclusions, we wonder whether something very fundamental about reality has been understood. At the very least, the dialogue is thought-provoking.

PATTERNS

Modern science has shown us that the universe ultimately transcends our rational, conscious intellect. Yet we can represent relationships within forces of the universe in symbols, which can translate into formulae, mathematical and geometrical patterns. As a result, we can predict, control, and transform matter in ways that until now could only be found in science fiction. The technology revolution now taking place is a direct result.

Physics theorist Werner Heisenberg discovered that when a particle is observed and measured, it changes. He determined that it was impossible to both measure energy and determine its location, an idea now known as the Heisenberg Uncertainty Principle. This has found its way into the general theory of knowledge. We will never be quite so certain of anything anymore.

Physics began to question whether it was possible to decide what the ultimate forces and constituents of matter really are. Should the threads that made up the fabric of the universe be thought of as tiny particles or as energy waves? Is a tiny particle the foundation or is it the relationship between particles, the pattern, that creates matter? We cannot say the answer is only one, offered the Danish scientist Niels Bohr, who originally proposed an important piece of atomic theory: complementarity. It is best to have both ways of thinking available. The basic essence may be thought of as either the particle or the wave, depending on your point of view and the needs of the moment. A group of trees, viewed from a distance, becomes a forest; close up, it consists of trees. An individual tree is both a tree and a part of the forest. The principle of complementarity is remarkably similar to a part of Madhyamika philosophy, which would reject both possibilities yet accept them as well. Truth is somewhere in between. Buddhist doctrine has been in accord with this for thousands of years.

As Western philosophy evolved to postmodernism, it became clear that all theory, all knowledge, is constructed. No philosophical position is certain, no theory is infallible. Our minds create what we experience through our perception, as the mandala would suggest. The more we know, the less we can be sure of. We learn how little we know of how much there is to know.

But like science, Tibetan Buddhism is hopeful. We can know, and be free of the narrow limits of illusion, by using correct methods. We can learn higher truths, which are patterns hidden within the nature of all that is, universal patterns of relationship. This is what great abstract artists like Wassily Kandinsky were getting at when they deleted the representational content from their art, instead giving us pure abstract patterns. Then more fundamental experience emerges.

This universal understanding that pattern is primary is what modern science recognizes and is even now searching to fill with experimentation. One of the great discoveries in modern science was the understanding of mechanisms. We have been dedicated as a culture to discovering what the mechanisms are in order to improve how things function. One area that has made great strides in understanding human applications of mechanism is neuroscience. One current theory is that each section of the brain is specialized for very specific tasks. Neuroscientists are striving to isolate and uncover specific mechanisms in the brain, believing that they will eventually be able to show that mind, consciousness, even spiritual experiences are the result of brain mechanisms. But the brain maps and remaps reality as needed. If a limb is lost, a new way of experiencing the body is soon created. Patterns are not fixed for all time.

But mechanisms also serve a purpose, and each has its place in the mandala. Co-existence of mind and brain is closer to the truth, according to the Dalai Lama. Inner patterns reflect outer form, and outer form reflects inner patterns. These patterns are connected to our minds in ways we do not fully understand, but continually use.

Western philosophy has made a distinction between form and content. But in Tibetan Buddhism, form is content and content is form. There is no form outside of the content, nor is there content without form. The two co-exist because of each other, in a circular relationship, without duality. Our best understandings from science show us that there is an underlying order to the universe, it is lawful, but not caused in a simple way. This mysterious relationship is a function of Oneness, of the nirvana we are all part of.

MIND ONLY PERCEIVES THE WORLD

Our senses give us an experience of reality that is related to that reality but is not literally the reality, as if it were shown in a mirror. The solid world, as we experience it, is only relatively so—a function of the limited range of our senses and measuring devices.

Our intelligence joins with the sensory data to construct an experienced world. Our minds create a permanent reality in conjunction with the illusion of constancy that we take for granted. We can look at a two-dimensional picture of the lines and planes of a room and get an experience of three-dimensional space. We see a person walking away from us get progressively smaller. We do not assume that the person got smaller. Instead, the size change is experienced as distance changing. We do not experience the inside of our house disappearing when we close the door; we know, instead, that it is simply no longer visible, but it is still there. Similarly, following enlightenment, everyday life does not disappear; simply, everyday reality is transformed. Nirvana and samsara are not separate. Experience shows the actual world as a sign of the enlightened spiritual world.

DIRECT PERCEPTION IS POSSIBLE

Scientific instruments have shown that the world of appearances is deceiving and that better perception is possible. By attuning the senses from simple experience to also include the symbolic level opens the doors of the mind to direct perception and, thus, greater potential. Engaging in transactions on the material level permits fulfillment and inner transformation on the spiritual level. Buddhism can help science to evolve further. As the practitioners of both explore their similarities and differences, a map appears to show the way to greater understanding. New discoveries will undoubtedly follow.

CHAPTER 15

Wisdom Through Love

> *Love, enjoyed by the ignorant,*
> *Becomes bondage.*
> *That very same love, tasted by one with understanding*
> *Brings liberation.*
> *Enjoy all the pleasures of love fearlessly,*
> *For the sake of liberation.*
> —*Cittavisuddhiprakarana Tantra*

DEVELOPING COMPASSIONATE RELATIONSHIPS

In recent years, psychologists have become interested in studying wisdom. Their conceptions of wisdom relate to excellence and high levels of functioning. Included in this list is also reference to compassionate feelings toward others. "Wisdom involves good intentions. It is used for the well-being of oneself and others" (Bates and Staudinger 2000, 123).

Wisdom is incomplete without compassion. According to the Dalai Lama, compassion *is* wisdom—there is no distinction between them. This implies that how we relate to others is integral to enlightenment. Day-to-day living expresses enlightened wisdom in action. Enlightenment is not a solitary experience; it happens in the midst of relationships. Open yourself correctly to your relationships and you will find lessons revealed in every interaction, all helping you to develop.

BECOMING RECEPTIVE TO LEARNING: GURU YOGA

Creating an open and receptive attitude makes wisdom possible. It is important to abandon attitudes that get in the way of positive relationships and to maintain attitudes that are receptive to them. These positive learning approaches can be generalized to other learning situations. Tibetan Buddhism is often learned under a guru. Guru Yoga teaches attitudes toward yourself, your guru, teacher, or therapist that make you receptive to others so that learning can be optimal. The exercises that follow are drawn from Guru Yoga.

Opening Yourself to Learning

You should be sincere and intense in your desire to develop your spiritual understanding. Strong desire, however, is not enough. Begin with your attitude toward yourself.

Sit quietly and allow yourself to reflect on how fortunate you are to be alive as a human being in a position to learn. "Take advantage of your extremely valuable human life—a life-form hard to find and once found, very meaningful" (Mullin 1982, 75). If you think you have deficits and disadvantages, consider them in relation to one who has less, or compare with an animal, a dog or cat, which does not even have the mental, physical, and emotional abilities you have. Try to understand how you are uniquely endowed with the aptitude to learn. Recognize that, as a human being, you are capable of turning away from the negative and toward the positive.

A group of teachings known as The Precious Rosary contains precepts of the gurus encouraging students to make certain efforts that will help them be successful in their endeavors. Students promise to direct themselves according to the best of their abilities. Incorporating these attitudes can be helpful in getting more out of appropriate learning situations. There are hundreds of different precepts, but here are some important ones to get you started.

Meditation on Attitudes to Foster Learning

Think about these qualities and try to adopt them in your everyday life. Be sincere in your efforts.

Allow yourself to feel intensely interested and motivated toward your spiritual development.

Keep your mind alert while going about every activity.

Apply your intelligence to notice the difference between actions that will benefit you on your path versus those that will lead you away from your path.

Abandon mistaken attitudes and behaviors. Maintain receptive ones.

Do not allow yourself to do anything that violates the Ten Commandments (if you are from the Judeo/Christian tradition) or comparable moral rules. Without making a sincere effort to live ethically, you cannot hope to find spiritual fulfillment.

Dealing with Resistance

As in all efforts to improve, people will have their ups and downs. Some faltering is natural and can be used as an opportunity to learn. If you find that you are not able to maintain positive attitudes for learning, do this meditation. Repeat it when necessary.

First be aware of how you have faltered. Notice what you did, thinking very carefully about how it came about and why you did it. Contemplate the shortcomings of negativity, such as how negative actions tend to lead to negative consequences, whereas positive actions lead to positive consequences. Allow yourself to feel sorry. Recognize that you are capable of improving your actions. Generate a strong sense of motivation to correct your actions in the future. Continue your meditation practice, which will help you to be more successful in the future.

ENHANCING RELATIONSHIPS

Learning to use your better instincts for the benefit of others can begin with the people closest to you. In some sects, practitioners traveled their path to self-development with a partner, sharing the journey to enlightenment together. These practices can bring passion and intimacy into your primary relationship.

Perform these meditations together with your partner.

Meditation on Mutuality

A relationship that best fosters personal transformation is for the mutual benefit of both people equally. Consider how you and your partner are on a shared journey through life. Think about ways that you can respect your partner's abilities, qualities, and potentials. Do you take your partner's interest into account for your own actions? Have empathy for the other person's feelings and take them as seriously as your own. Recognize that both partners receive mutual benefit by fostering each other.

Imagining the Other

Mutuality may seem like a positive ideal to strive toward, but some may find it difficult to actualize. Sometimes it is not easy to step beyond your own ego to think of your partner's feelings and needs. This meditation helps to bridge the gap.

Switch places with your partner by imagining that you are your partner. Think of a typical situation that you and your partner share. Visualize yourself with all the thoughts and feelings that your partner would be likely to have in this situation. Feel the reality of this perspective for the other, just as real as yours is to you. Can you allow this to become a part of you? Discuss what you each felt in switching. What do you learn about yourself and each other?

OPENNESS

In a mutual relationship, both partners should be honest, sensitive, and responsive to each other. Each person enters the interaction with open awareness. They must both be willing to share experiences. Through their closeness they develop deep intimacy.

Mindful Meditation on Openness

Turn your attention to your relationship. Are you open with your partner? Meditate on your interactions. If you notice that you are not being open, ask yourself why. Is the problem coming from you? If you are holding back, question yourself. Become aware of what you say, think, and feel as you interact. Do you feel that your partner is not sharing with you? If you feel that the openness is not mutual, discuss it with your partner. Mutual trust is primary in having an open relationship.

Enlightened Passion

Tantricism embraces our emotional nature and uses it as a pathway to enlightenment. You can be mindfully aware even in the midst of strong emotions. Developing the ability to feel what you feel without losing awareness can help you cope better with life in general. Practice this meditation alone at first, and then try it in the midst of an emotional situation.

Sit quietly and imagine a time when you felt a strong emotion. Begin with a happy time. Visualize all the details until you begin to have the feelings you had at the time. As you do, maintain your awareness, notice what you feel but do not make value judgments or assessments. Simply experience the feelings.

When you are comfortable with this meditation, try practicing your awareness in a real situation. As you begin to feel emotion, meditate on the feeling, just as you meditated on an object in Chapter 11. Keep your awareness on this experience as you feel. Do not interfere with the experience; let it evolve. Maintain your awareness without making value judgments, such as this is a stupid feeling or you love this feeling. Simply be at One with the experience, and continue to act maturely. You can try this meditation with many different feelings.

Meditation on Sexual Intimacy

Sexual union is the expression of intimacy. The sexual act is performed with caring concern for the pleasure of the other. At the moment of climax, people feel a melting of the personal ego that is not unlike the transcending of self experienced in enlightenment. The practice of meditation even during sex can not only enhance your experience of sexual intimacy but also brings you closer to enlightenment.

Throughout the experience, both partners should practice meditation. Maintain clear, moment-to-moment awareness, experience deeply. Feel your compassion and love for your partner. Give your partner pleasure as you open yourself to receiving it as well. Meditate on what you feel, the sensations and emotions for the other. Keep your mind focused and alert, as you have trained yourself to do, so that the moment of climax can be both blissful and empty at the same time.

PROBLEM-SOLVING CONFLICTS IN RELATIONSHIPS

When you live with enlightenment, your world takes on the universal perspective of compassion and caring for all. You can see the failings in yourself and others leading away from enlightenment. Conflict with other people is often related to confusion of levels. The absolute level of enlightenment has no conflict because it is beyond conflict. Relationship to others can be improved by including the absolute dimension. Problems dissolve in the new context.

Gurus invite their students to transcend, to switch levels. The everyday relationship requires at times remaining in or communicating through the relative levels. Whenever possible, evoke the absolute, the non-situational. Conflicts may be resolved by switching levels. The relative level of identity, as an everyday person, may conflict with the others, but the absolute identity never does.

A deity may have qualities that the everyday person lacks, and taking on the role of the deity may provide new insights and potentials. All these are merely expedient means of enlightenment. The true self is beyond this or any concept. But sometimes, relative level conflicts hold us back. We believe we must deal with them to free ourselves. Buddhism denies their ultimate reality. Conflict is an opportunity to practice selfless altruism, to learn. Practice of the guru's precepts is close to enlightenment; indeed, it is a function of it. The guru speaks to us and through us, when we enter the mandala of our personal transformation. We cannot hope to evolve without doing so. There is a source of values within.

Join to the center, weave together the threads of samsara (relative) and nirvana (absolute). Enlightened relationships then become possible.

DEVELOPING COMPASSION FOR THE WORLD

Compassion does not stop with your primary partner or your immediate circle of family and friends. It should extend to all of humanity. The Seven-Point Oral Tradition is a step-by-step method to develop your feelings of compassion for the entire world. Drawn from Serlinga, Atisa's teacher, these ancient methods were carried forward by the first and third Dalai Lamas. They called them the "lojang teachings." Our current Dalai Lama believes these teachings have been essential to his personal development:

> *I myself received the lojang teachings when still a child, and have used them as the basis for my practice since that time. I include lojang methods of meditation*

for cultivating the spirit of love and compassion in my own daily devotions and have greatly benefited from them. (Dalai Lama in Druppa 1993, 13)

The method offers a perspective to try out through contemplation. Think about the ideas. Let yourself play with the possibilities and consequences of taking this position.

Equanimity Meditation

You can "warm up" to the seven-point method with this meditation. First, think of the neutral people in your life: those you do not know personally who have neither helped nor hurt you in any way. Try to generate a feeling of calm and composure about them. This probably will not be too difficult. Now try imagining someone you are very close to. Try to develop a calm, composed attitude toward this person. Next, think about someone who has angered you. Can you allow yourself to feel calm composure about him or her?

Seven-Point Tradition Meditation

Begin by imagining that all people in the world have been your mother. Tibetan Buddhists argue that because we have all been reborn countless times, everyone has been our mother at one time or another. From this logic comes the idea that you will inevitably be a mother, too.

Consider how your mother showed you kindness. For example, in the womb, she protected you. As an infant, she wrapped you in soft blankets, held you in her arms, smiled at you, and fed you.

Some people may have mixed feelings about how their mothers raised them. Realize that mothers, like all human beings who are unenlightened, suffer from immaturity, problems, and conflicts. Think about trying to help your mother, and all mothers, transcend their difficulties and find happiness. In order to help someone else, you must mature in your own life. Thus, make the effort to develop yourself for the benefit of the world.

These practices are a solution to how virtue can be taught. We may not have always been compassionate and kind in our lives, but we can develop these qualities at any point. As you make efforts toward more compassionate living, you create a more humane world for yourself. Enter the mandala of compassion and enjoy the life it brings.

CHAPTER 16

Transformation Through the Great Symbol

Taking your own body and mind as the laboratory, see if you can use these different techniques: that is to say, engage in some thorough-going research on your own mental functioning, and examine the possibility of making some positive changes within yourself.
—His Holiness the Dalai Lama

SANCTIFYING LIFE

If the phenomena of the world are the great symbol, sign of higher reality, then all the experiences of life are symbolic and can be utilized in the service of tantric living. Body movements, imagery, and gestures can become the first steps to transformation.

The source of patterned imagery can be external or internal. Everything that takes place, whether outside or within you, is an opportunity to learn and practice. The important point is that each life is symbolic. Enlightenment is continuously expressed in symbols. If we harmonize with the Great Symbol in our own lives, we return to contact with the source, the well-spring of transformation.

Order is intrinsic to the universe; images and sounds are an expression of these underlying patterns. We are part of a larger mind that includes us; our lives are meaningful in both a personal and transpersonal sense, part of a pattern beyond the possibility of our conscious conception. Perceive directly, beyond concepts. Use your consciousness to relate to and enter the symbolic realm, to perceive reality as it is. Then much more becomes possible.

Emotional reactions can be used as an opportunity to practice correct attitudes. According to the doctrine, there are positive attitudes and negative attitudes, correct ways to respond and incorrect ways to respond. Correct ways lead deeper into the dharma, to the center of the mandala. Incorrect ways and attitudes lead away from the dharma and out of the mandala. This is an important distinction concerning the direction of the path. Cultivating your attitudes can transform this life. Your life-experiences are the grounds for entering the symbolic.

Discovering Symbols Exercise

Sit quietly in meditation. Close your eyes and focus your attention using the one-pointed awareness exercises from Chapter 11. When you feel relaxed and undistracted, turn the light of your awareness toward your sensations. For example, pay attention to your muscles. Which ones are relaxed; which ones are tight? Do you begin to sense a pattern? Perhaps the muscles around your neck are tight, but all the other muscles are relaxed. Expand your observation. How is this pattern symbolic? Can you see connections? Does it represent fighting against forces? Start with your immediate experiencing. Any physical symptom, emotional reaction, or thought pattern can become your topic for meditation to learn about yourself and make positive changes.

Tibetans have their symbols; we have ours. The process is more important than its content. Symbolizing meaningfully is the center, not just the outer form of the symbols. Meaning is not necessarily dependent on form. Content is not form, but form includes content. Forms can give us information about all kinds of things, through meanings given to the symbols and by relationships between the objects and symbols. Thus, you can use your own symbolic sources if they are meaningful or vital to you. Your thinking can be stimulated by meditation on these symbols.

Finding Significance Exercise

You can take the smallest, most seemingly insignificant task and make it useful, symbolic of enlightenment. Pick something you do regularly, perhaps even without thinking, such as dusting your furniture or shoveling dirt in your garden. Become vividly aware of every movement you make. Imagine that each particle of dust or pile of dirt you remove is removing illusion from your mind. The more you dust or shovel, the clearer your perception becomes. You can adapt this to other tasks as well.

TRANSFORMING THROUGH EMOTIONS

Activities that are graceful, heroic, terrifying
Compassionate, furious, and peaceful—
And passion, anger, greed, pride, and envy—
All these things without exception
Are the perfected forms
Of pure well-illuminating wisdom.
(Shaw 1994a, 28)

Mahamudra teaches a profound principle of perception: be nonattached while permitting feelings and reactions. Use passions and emotions as tools of deeper insight to transcend them. The Dalai Lama has said that these methods can be adapted to modern therapy and the quest for inner change (Komito 1983, 4).

All phenomena and experiences are meaningful patterns, existing just as they are. Paradoxically, they are also without true, objective content. There are no actual objects. The deeper meaning of experience is its lack of one ultimate meaning. The meaning is the pattern, and the pattern is in its use. For example, a rechargeable battery cell is a physical pattern of electricity that looks like a cylinder or a rectangle. Each battery has charge capacities. Batteries also have an electronic memory that is largely a function of the pattern of charge and discharge. This memory will determine how much charging and discharging each battery will take, regardless of the standard for that type of battery. The cell takes on a mechanized learning-memory, based in the regular patterns of charge and discharge. In a very definite sense, the battery exhibits meaningful characteristics as a result of the patterning. This is also true of other aspects of our world. At many levels, emotional patterns are taken for granted. Once we recognize that we are all part of larger patterns, we can learn from them and evolve. We not only learn, as Gregory Bateson points out, we also learn how to learn. We free ourselves from our individual, narrow patterns of reaction by enlarging our patterns.

Meditation on Emotions

Your emotional reactions can be a springboard to more enlightened reactions. Sit quietly in meditation and focus. When you feel ready, turn your attention to your feelings. As you have a feeling, notice it with awareness. If you feel sadness, for example, allow yourself to feel it fully, but do not become swamped by it either. As the Mahamudra teaches, follow the threads of consciousness but do not leave it too loose or pull it too tight. By following and accepting your feeling, it naturally begins to transform, to evolve. Repeat this meditation at other times and you can enlarge your perspective to include different feeling-tones.

HEALING TRANSFORMATIONS:
BODY AWARENESS AND ENERGY WORK

Tibetan medicine includes Buddhist philosophy in its treatment of illnesses. We are vulnerable to disease because of the inevitable presence in unenlightened daily life of the factors known in Buddhism as the "three poisons": anger, attachment, and ignorance. We could think of the three poisons as spiritual stressors, but illness comes about from imbalances in terms of lifestyle, diet, conduct, and/or physiology. Remedies carefully crafted for each individual restore the correct balance of the factors of healthy functioning. The remedies can include combinations of herbs, meditation, and Kum Nye exercises, along with changes in diet, lifestyle, conduct, and attitude. All of these are prescribed with the wisdom born of correct medical training and the essential ingredient from the doctor: compassion.

Kum Nye is a method of enhancing body awareness through sequences of movements with focused attention and emotion. The Nyingma are notable in systematizing the movements, but there are hundreds of traditional and modern possibilities.

Body awareness and experiential movement exercises are ancient, originally used in many philosophies. Bodhidharma, the legendary founder of Zen Buddhism, transmitted Zen to the monks of the Shaolin Temple with a set of exercise movements, the I-Chin-Ching. Modern psychotherapy methods from Alexander Lowen, Wilhelm Reich, and an extension of his approach called Bioenergetics use variations of postures, breathing, and movements that are consistent with this theory, that body and mind are one. Changes in the mind can be evoked by changes in the body. Lowen believed that energy is blocked by patterns of defensive, chronic tensions of the muscles. Specific exercises with stretching and breathing while focusing attention can activate the individual life force, energizing and freeing its passage through the body. This affects the person's whole experience, resulting in transformation. Tibetan holistic medicine integrates these practices into their healing prescriptions.

Kum Nye Exercises
Standing Meditation

Close your eyes and meditate for a few moments with arms resting at your sides. Lift your arms out from your sides and up until they are stretched high above your head. Imagine your body becoming lighter, as if your hands are being pulled upward by a strong balloon. Let your body expand as you breathe comfortably. Hold for a few minutes and then slowly bring your hands back down to your sides. Finish with your hands clasped together over your chest. Meditate quietly. Repeat the exercise several times.

Front HAH Exercise

Sit cross-legged or in a half lotus on a meditation pillow if possible, otherwise sit on a stool. Begin with your fists closed and touching each other in front of your chest. Press lightly as you inhale deeply and hold your breath. Then, in a single, vigorous motion, move your arms straight out, sideways, and open your hands, as you shout "HAH." Close your hands into fists again and return them to your chest. Repeat this exercise nine times in sets of three.

AWARENESS WHILE SLEEPING: LUCID DREAMING

Dreams offer another opportunity for growth and transformation in Tibetan Buddhism. The dream state is natural. We spend at least a third of our lives asleep, and much of that time is spent dreaming. Tibetan Buddhists encourage us to use that time to practice awareness for our transformation. Buddhism points out what folk wisdom says in the song lyrics "Row, row, row your boat . . . life is but a dream." Dreams offer the opportunity to awaken from the dream by becoming aware that we are dreaming.

Dreams are creative expressions of archetypes, and thereby hold a key to the transformational process. The study of significant symbols puts us in touch with deeper meanings. Dream Yoga focuses on the everyday experience as a symbol, part of a dream, and leads past the boundary of sleep versus waking. By interpreting life as a dream, we can lead ourselves into a different way of perceiving.

Dreams can be used to interpret through the unconscious, rather than the conscious. The conscious is used to show the unconscious symbolic awareness of the Clear Light of Buddha mind. Freud's famous statement, "Where id was there ego shall be," becomes "Where ego was, there Buddha mind shall be."

Lucid Dreaming 1

Anytime is a good time to develop your meditative mind. Lucid Dreaming begins when you are awake. Consider how life is like a dream. Time passes. When you think back on what you were doing ten years ago, it probably seems like a dream.

When you are awake, everything that transpires involves your mental experience of it. You have probably noticed that you can be aware of yourself when awake if you deliberately apply meditation techniques. Recognize the dreamlike and mental qualities to waking life, exercise clear awareness during the day by applying meditation to everything you do. This can prepare you to extend your meditation to when you are asleep.

Lucid Dreaming 2

Dreams also arise from your mind. Realizing that dreams are illusions that arise from your mind, you can become aware of them. Resolve before you go to sleep that you would like to expand your meditation into dream consciousness. Say to yourself that tonight you would like to have many clear dreams and to be able to recognize the dream as a dream. With practice, you will become aware of your dreams while you are dreaming. Note them down.

Lucid Dreaming 3

Highly evolved practitioners can alter their dreams as they choose. This advanced technique may be beyond you at the early stages of practice, but you can learn to influence your dreams in a positive direction. As you lie in bed in that relaxed state between waking and sleeping, calm your mind.

Just as you drift off to sleep, imagine a beautiful lotus flower (or any flower you like). Vividly picture it as you begin drifting off to sleep. Then imagine that you are floating in the center of the flower, lulled comfortably to sleep. This experience of perfect peace, empty of everything else, can help you to blend meditation with sleep.

IMAGINING AS REAL: DEITY YOGA

This is a psychic world, not just a physical world. There is no real, objective thought that cannot, at times, be pushed out of our awareness by an unreal, subjective one. The subjective world of thought and experience—consciousness—is not merely a function of material causes in the brain. Consciousness is grounded in the spiritual, and this can be enhanced by imaginative methods.

Higher consciousness is possible when you can let go of the context of an external point of view. Visualization involves becoming One with the concept, entering the experience, losing yourself in the process of total immersion. Visualization in the psychic world leads to experiences and events in the actual material world. They are not separate. A process of meaningful relationships infinitely links images and symbols in time and space. Jung (1973) defined these links as noncausal synchronicity. Sometimes things happen together even if one does not cause the other. These non-causal threads make up the tapestry of the mandala. As you get in touch with these interconnections and permit them, you find harmony with the inner, deeper symbols of transformation.

In Deity Yoga, you practice meditating on the deity or buddha, the ultimate symbol of transformation, contemplate deeply until you can experience that you are the deity or buddha. By doing this you form a noncausal link. You come to realize that the self is an illusion, just as the deity you are imagining is an illusion. The attributes of the deities, paradoxically, become your own.

We play many roles in life as part of the natural expression of Shakespeare's dictum "All the world's a stage, And all the men and women merely players." We all have our entrances and our exits. Deity Yoga has taught this great truth for thousands of years.

Role-playing is a time-honored way to learn and try out experiences and behaviors. You can play any role and set up any situation to see how the different roles interact. Links are formed so that change can happen.

Certain visualizations and traditional dramatic interchanges make transformation possible. As the *Tibetan Book of the Dead* points out, you are the deity. When you realize this, the image disappears and you are left with your pure, enlightened being—the goal of the practice. In a therapeutic sense, Deity Yoga is used to explore your life and its possibilities. Reality may be limited, but imagination does not need to be.

Meditation on Your Spiritual Guide

This classic meditation comes from Deity Yoga. Sit quietly and close your eyes. If you have a teacher, imagine your teacher is sitting before you. If not, imagine buddha sitting before you as your teacher. Your teacher is wise and compassionate. Try to visualize him or her clearly, sitting face-to-face, with a kindly expression, warmly communicating to you. Imagine this guru encouraging you in a calm, powerful, penetrating voice, "Practice! Keep meditating! Stay on your Path!" Meditate on the guru's beneficial function in your spiritual life.

You Are the Buddha

As you progress along your journey, you learn through meditation that the wisdom and compassion of buddha can be evoked within you. You have the same capacities as the greatest buddhas and bodhisattvas of all times. Zen Buddhists express this idea when they say that we all have buddha mind.

Think of all the wonderful qualities of Buddha—his great wisdom and deep compassion. Imagine that you have these qualities and that you live them in everyday life. What would you be like? Vividly visualize yourself living wisely, with love and caring for others. Focus on your feelings about it. Open yourself to your highest potentials—these abilities are already there, waiting to be awakened and used. Allow yourself to transform, to become the best you can be, living fully in harmony with the Great Symbol!

CONCLUSION

Life offers us a great opportunity to become enlightened and live a happy, fulfilled existence in accord with higher truth. Every action we engage in and every relationship we have has the potential to give us meaningful experiences to learn from, to grow in our wisdom and compassionate understanding. Often we do not know what we have until we no longer have it.

The end of the path we are on is only the beginning. The wheel of time is turning; propelling us toward an enlightened destiny that will include all in the great sea of nirvana. Wise ones are watching over us, extending a helping hand everywhere. We can learn from others regardless of their imperfections if we learn to perceive the realm of the symbolic here in the realm of the actual. We should recognize this truth now, and not miss it. We are fortunate to be given this moment in time. Let us use it wisely and well!

> *We wonder as we wander*
> *Throughout this world*
> *Of tragic strife*
> *What is the answer to*
> *The problems of life*
> *The timeless answers*
> *To our inner call*
> *Love will transform us*
> *One and all.*
> —C. Alexander Simpkins

BIBLIOGRAPHY

Anderson, Walt. 1980. Open Secrets: A Western guide to Tibetan Buddhism. Middlesex, England: Penguin Books.

Arnheim, Rudolf. 1966. *Toward a Psychology of Art*. Berkeley: University of California Press.

———. 1969. *Visual Thinking*. Berkeley: University of California Press.

Bates, Paul B., and Ursula M. Staudinger. 2000. "Wisdom: A Metaheuristic (Pragmatic) to Orchestrate Mind and Virtue Toward Excellence." *American Psychologist* 55, no. 1 (January): 122–36.

Bernbaum, Edwin. 1980. *The Way to Shambhala*. Garden City, N.Y.: Anchor Press/Doubleday.

Bharati, Agehananda. 1970. *The Tantric Tradition*. London: Rider & Company.

Chattopadhyaya, Alaka. 1967. *Atisa and Tibet*. Calcutta: R.D. Press

Druppa, Gyalwa Gendun. 1993. *Training the Mind in the Great Way*. Ithaca, N.Y.: Snow Lion Publications.

Eliade, Mircea. 1987. *The Sacred & the Profane: The Nature of Religion*. San Diego, Calif.: Harcourt Brace Jovanovich.

Evans-Wentz, Walter Y. 1954. *The Tibetan Book of the Great Liberation*. London: Oxford University Press.

———. 1960. *The Tibetan Book of the Dead*. London: Oxford University Press.

———. 1967. *Tibetan Yoga and Secret Doctrines*. London: Oxford University Press.

———. 1981. *Cuchama and Sacred Mountains*. Chicago: Swallow Press.

Freke, Timothy. 1998. *The Wisdom of the Tibetan Lamas*. Boston: Tuttle Publishing.

Govinda, Lama Anagarika. 1970. *Foundations of Tibetan Mysticism*. London: Rider & Company. Gyaltsen, Kenpo Konchog. 1990. *The Great Kagyu Masters*. Ithaca, N.Y.: Snow Lion Publications.

Gyatrul, Rinpoche, Jigme Tenpe Nyima, Lochen Dharma Shri, and His Highness Dudjom Rinpoche. 1993. *Ancient Wisdom: Nyingma Teachings on Dream Yoga, Meditation and Transformation*. Ithaca, N.Y.: Snow Lion Publications.

Gyatso, Tenzin. 1990. *Freedom in Exile: The Autobiography of the Dalai Lama*. New York: HarperCollins Publishers.

———. 1995. *The World of Tibetan Buddhism*. Boston: Wisdom Publications.

Hayward, Jeremy W., and J. Varela Francisco. 1992. *Gentle Bridges: Conversations with the Dalai Lama on the Sciences of Mind*. Boston: Shambhala Publications.

Heisenberg, Werner. 1975. *Across the Frontiers*. New York: Harper Torchbooks.

Heller, Amy. 1999. *Tibetan Art: Tracing the Development of Spiritual Ideals and Art in Tibet 600-2000 A.D.* Milan, Italy: Editoriale Jaca Book SpA.

Hoffman, Helmut. 1961. *The Religions of Tibet*. New York: Macmillan.

Houshmand, Zara, Robert B. Livingston, and B. Alan Wallace. 1999. *Consciousness at the Crossroads: Conversations with the Dalai Lama on Brain Science and Buddhism*. Ithaca, N.Y.: Snow Lion Publications.

Jung, Carl G. 1977. *Collective Unconscious*. Princeton, N.J.: Princeton University Press.

———. 1966. *Two Essays on Analytical Psychology*. Princeton, N.J.: Princeton University Press.

————. 1973. *Synchronicity*. Princeton, N.J.: Princeton University Press.

————. 1980. *The Archetypes and the Collective Unconscious*. Princeton, N.J.: Princeton University Press.

————. 1981. *The Structure and Dynamics of the Psyche*. Princeton, N.J.: Princeton University Press.

————. 1981. *Man and His Symbols*. New York: Anchor Books/Doubleday.

Klein, Anne C. 1998. *Knowledge and Liberation*. Ithaca, N.Y.: Snow Lion Publication.

Komito, David Ross. 1983. "Tibetan Buddhism and psychotherapy: A conversation with the Dalai Lama." *Journal of Transpersonal Psychology* 15, no. 1: 1–13.

Lessing, F. D. , and A. Wayman. 1978. *Introduction to the Buddhist Tantric Systems*. Delhi: Motilal Banarsidass.

Lopez, Donald S., Jr., ed. 1997. *Religions of Tibet in Practice*. Princeton, N.J.: Princeton University Press.

Lowry, John. 1973. *Tibetan Art*. London: Her Majesty's Stationery Office.

Mullin, Glenn H. 1982. *The Path to Enlightenment: H.H. the Dalai Lama*. Ithaca, N.Y.: Snow Lion Publications.

Pal, Pratapaditya. 1969. *The Art of Tibet*. Boston: The Asia Society, Inc.

Powers, John. 1995. *Introduction to Tibetan Buddhism*. Ithaca, N.Y.: Snow Lion Publications.

Reed, Stephen K. 1996. *Cognition: Theory and Application*. Pacific Grove, Calif.: Brooks/Cole Publishing Company.

Revel, Jean-Francois, and Matthieu Ricard. 1998. *The Monk and the Philosopher*. New York: Schocken Books.

Reynolds, Valrae. 1999. *From the Sacred Realm*. Munich: Prestel.

Sangpo, Rinpochay Khetsun. 1982. *Tantric Practice in Nying-ma*. London: Rider.

Schlagintweit, Emil. (1863) 1968. *Buddhism in Tibet*. London: Susil Gupta.

Shaw, Miranda. 1994a. *Passionate Enlightenment: Women in Tantric Buddhism*. Princeton, N.J.: Princeton University Press.

————. 1994b. "Liberating Sexuality: Miranda Shaw talks about tantra." *Tricycle, The Buddhist Review* 1994c (Summer). Vol. 3 #4,

Simpkins, C. Alexander, and Annellen M. Simpkins. 2000. *Simple Buddhism: A Guide to Enlightened Living.* Boston: Tuttle Publishing.

————. 1999. *Simple Zen: A Guide to Living Moment by Moment.* Boston: Tuttle Publishing.

————. 1998. *Meditation from Thought to Action.* Boston: Tuttle Publishing.

————. 1997. *Zen Around the World: 2500 Years from the Buddha to You.* Boston: Tuttle Publishing.

————. 1997. *Living Meditation: From Principle to Practice.* Boston: Tuttle Publishing.

————. 1996. *Principles of Meditation: Eastern Wisdom for the Western Mind.* Boston: Tuttle Publishing.

Singer, Jane Casey, and Philip Denwood. 1997. *Tibetan Art: Towards a Definition of Style.* London: Lawrence King Publishing.

Snellgrove, David. 1987. *Indo-Tibetan Buddhism,* Vol. I and II. Boston: Shambhala.

Sopa, Geshe Lhundup, and Jeffrey Hopkins. 1976. *Practice and Theory of Tibetan Buddhism.* New York: Grove Press.

Standing, Lionel. 1973. "Learning 10,000 pictures." *Quarterly Journal of Expermental Psychology* 25: 207–222.

Thondup, Tulku. 1996. *Masters of Meditation and Miracles.* Boston: Shambhala.

Thurman, Robert A. F. 1995. *Essential Tibetan Buddhism.* New York: Harper San Francisco.

————, trans. 1994. *The Tibetan Book of the Dead.* New York: Bantam Books.

Trungpa, Chogyam. 1994. *Illusion's Game: The Life and Teaching of Naropa.* Boston: Shambhala.

Tulku, Tarthang, ed. 1975. *Reflections of Mind: Western Psychology Meets Tibetan Buddhism.* Emeryville, Calif.: Dharma Publishing.

Waddell, L. Austine. 1894. *The Buddhism of Tibet or Lamaism*. Cambridge, England: W. Heffer and Sons Limited.

Wayman, Alex, trans. 1978. *Calming the Mind and Discerning the Real: Buddhist Meditation and the Middle View from the Lam rim chen mo of Tsong Kha pa*. New York: Columbia University Press.

Wicks, Robert. 1997. "The Therapeutic Psychology of the *Tibetan Book of the Dead*." *Philosophy, East and West* 47, no. 4 (October).

Willis, Janice, ed. 1995. *Feminine Ground: Essays on Women and Tibet*. Ithaca, N.Y.: Snow Lion Publications.

Library of Congress Cataloging-in-Publication Data

Simpkins, C. Alexander.
    Simple Tibetan Buddhism : a guide to Tantric living. / by C. Alexander Simpkins &
    Annellen Simpkins.-- 1st ed.
        p. cm.
    Includes bibliographical references.
    ISBN 0-8048-3199-8 (pb.)
        1. Buddhism--China--Tibet. 2. Religious life--Tantric Buddhism. I. Simpkins,
Annellen M. II. Title.

BQ7612 .S56 2001
294.3'923--dc21   2001035551

ALSO BY C. ALEXANDER AND ANNELLEN SIMPKINS

Principles of Meditation

•

Zen Around the World

•

Living Meditation

•

Meditation from Thought to Action

•

Simple Taoism

•

Simple Zen

•

Simple Confucianism

•

Simple Buddhism

•

Self-Hypnosis Plain & Simple